No Longer Sick

No Longer Sick

A Young Man's Struggle with Chronic Illness

Allison Greene

To Susan —
my friend for
20+ years!
♡2you!

Allison Greene

RESOURCE *Publications* · Eugene, Oregon

NO LONGER SICK
A Young Man's Struggle with Chronic Illness

Resource Publications
An Imprint of Wipf and Stock Publishers
199 W. 8th Ave., Suite 3
Eugene, OR 97401

www.wipfandstock.com

PAPERBACK ISBN: 978-1-6667-9779-4
HARDCOVER ISBN: 978-1-6667-9778-7
EBOOK ISBN: 978-1-6667-9780-0

VERSION NUMBER 022322

"Frequently Asked Questions" copyright Keith Superdock, MD, transplant nephrologist. Used with permission.

Special thanks to writers' group members Jeanne Brooks, Wanda Owings, Deb Richardson-Moore, and Susan Simmons; to critical readers Jennifer Childs, Vic Greene, Wendy Harman, Dejan Lukovic, Elaine Nocks, Liv Osby, Emily Price, Megan Greene Roberts, and Jen Walsh; to Martin Crane and Andre LaCroix for their anonymous inclusions; to Shea Garbett for her help in preparing photos; to my family and close friends—you know who you are and that I wouldn't have made it without you; to Jon Tuttle for his encouragement; and to special practitioners Melissa Palmer-Hernandez, NP, Carlos Zayas, MD, and nurse Doug.

The account that follows reflects a mother's frustrations over a long, difficult journey and does not intend to impugn any health care provider or facility.

John Garrison Greene
October 2, 1983—July 23, 2020

I struggle and arise

Contents

Introduction

I HAD A BEAUTIFUL son. Such a simple sentence and yet so full of complexity.

John entered my life as an unplanned embryo in the winter of 1983. It was not a convenient time. His dad was finishing up a doctoral program. We were both working part time in hospitals and managing our two-year-old daughter. I was also taking an early morning art class at a local college. While I never wanted to have an only child, I had just told myself that we should wait until Megan was five, even though the books said three years was the perfect age span. John had other ideas.

Initially he fulfilled my art teacher's class assignment to depict a "blue intruder."

He fulfilled so much more than that. At three weeks old, after we'd finally moved back home to South Carolina, he filled the space in my heart when my father died. Unlike his colicky sister, John was such a sweet baby. He cried when he was hungry, smiled up at me, and went back to sleep. No child could have been more loved. By all of us, even his sister who remembers sitting on him when he tried to crawl.

John died on July 23, 2020, at age thirty-six with his dog Pippen beside him. After a ten-year struggle with End Stage Renal Disease following a rare autoimmune disease, he is no longer sick.

Together John and I wrote, *Since John Got Sick* (Wipf and Stock Publishers, 2018). I never knew he could write—he was always outside with a ball in his hands. He wrote all his parts on his cell phone during the many nights he couldn't sleep. I wish for his help writing the rest of his story. I need his sardonic wit lest readers have to slough through my sad telling. I even tried writing his parts anyway, as a voice from beyond, but my daughter said he would hate anyone trying to do that. She is probably right, so his words from remembered conversations will have to suffice. I hope you will read his own words in our previous book, as well as those of his friends found in the Tributes section of this one.

In April 2010 John was diagnosed with Wegener's granulomatosis (or GPA). As detailed in our earlier book, John was always healthy until the age of twenty-six when he was suddenly admitted directly from the emergency room to the intensive care unit. A few years out of college then, he had a job, a girlfriend, and friends—always friends.

The disease, determined to be "idiopathic" or without known cause, caused him to hemorrhage internally, particularly with his lungs bleeding out. For four months he received countless blood transfusions and toxic medications while in an induced coma with a machine breathing for him. He should have died multiple times, yet he did not.

After those four months of hospitalization and relearning how to swallow, speak, sit, walk, and eat again, he came home to live with me, with the hope that the disease was in remission and all could be well. "Get my life back on track," he said. But three weeks later, the disease destroyed his kidney function and he was readmitted to the hospital in renal failure. That time we got the diagnosis of End Stage Renal Disease.

I think now that at some deep level, I perceived the finality in that diagnosis. Yet I had seen him defy death multiple times. We pushed on for a solution.

The solution involved three more hospitalizations that fall with three unsuccessful vascular surgery attempts to get adequate access for dialysis. Also, John started dialysis (still without good access) which he did for twenty-one months. That December 2010 brought a return hospital trip to Duke University Medical Center for a second round of infusions to get the Wegener's back in remission. Two more vascular surgeries, these at Duke in the first half of 2011, achieved a working "fistula." We continued to have hope—specifically for a kidney transplant.

Since John Got Sick tracks our journey over the next few years. During that time, he and I were approved for a kidney transplantation. John described his struggles that followed: depression, financial insecurity, prescription opioid withdrawal, and inability to live the life he'd dreamed of. I recounted the weight of being a care partner for a strong-willed young man, along with providing financial support and managing a demanding job.

This current story focuses on the last fifteen months of John's life (May 2019—July 2020), seven years after transplant and nine years since John first got sick. This is my story, too, of our relationship and my perception of his experience (along with review of the medical record). Honestly, there are not a lot of happy moments in this narrative. John was so ill in so many complex ways and struggled so hard to overcome them.

I want to share our story with any parent who has lost a child, with anyone who has End Stage Renal Disease or autoimmune disorders, and for all those a experiencing a complex health journey whether as a patient or a caregiver. While the primary medical focus of this story is kidney disease, John's illness was so much more than the physical disease. It was also mental, emotional, and spiritual, as any life-threatening disease surely must be. I want to bring awareness to this vulnerable population.

Mostly, I want to honor a brave young man for his valiant fight.

A writer friend of mine, encouraging me in this effort, said, "You have to write him back to life." Others have maybe done a better job with that than I in sharing their memories. (See Tributes.) I saw his struggles, and I don't want that life for him again.

I realized as I progressed that I am writing myself back to life, too. I gave so much of myself to John those ten years, and especially the last hellacious fifteen months, that there seems little left of me but a shell.

An acquaintance of John's wrote me after his death:

> In my mind, John was a movie.
> I knew John from a distance as a kind of high school legend who participated in a life I could only dream about. He seemed blessed with everything a high schooler could want. He was smart, athletic, charming. I have several images of him etched in my memory of my high school years.
> Sometime after he first got sick, I reached out to him when a director friend of mine was researching about high school in the South, specifically the way different cultures and races came together. I immediately thought of John. He was really thoughtful in his response and sent me stories about some of the wilder things he got into in high school and right after. I remember thinking I could read a whole book of him telling stories.
> Last year I read Since John Got Sick in one sitting. My thirty-year-old cousin was fighting a rare cancer. Reading that book helped me understand what she and her mom were going through, but moreover, it felt cathartic to bear witness to John and what he'd written.

He came through to me as a person thrown into an impossible struggle, but who nevertheless faced it with a steely resolve. It takes a lot of guts to write about fear in such honest and straightforward language. I hope I could be so tough and so open.

Nothing came of my friend's movie idea. I tried to tell him about the epic arc of John's life, but I don't think he ever got it.

To me, John's life was indeed a movie, filled with both tragedy and triumph.

John, age 2

I

July 22, 2020

"THAT'S WHEN YOU WANT to go ahead and tuck your pants into your boots. Those suckers are everywhere," John commented while passing a worker opening a manhole in downtown Charleston. He knew his sister Megan would get the reference to roaches and the summer he worked laying sewer pipe. Nervous as usual, the patient was the one cracking the jokes as he was about to enter the hospital for a heart procedure, the last step in his journey for a second kidney transplant.

The previous day started rough. John was delayed in beginning his dialysis until he could stop throwing up. His girlfriend Jennifer reported to us it was because he was that nervous.

We–Megan, John, and I–had left Greenville around 2:30 and gotten to our friend's beach house around 7 p.m. We'd stopped to pick up seafood at a favorite spot and eaten it at her table, just like all the many times before when we'd shared beach trips as our families grew. For that evening our lives felt "normal," the way they used to be a long time ago. After dinner, John and Megan went for a walk on the beach. I hung back, my intent of the trip. I was worn down from John's long illness and my work, and when Megan offered to take this trip, my fourth in three months, I was grateful. Still, I had to be here. John could die and she would need me.

My boss in marketing for many years used to always tell us during times of high stress, "We aren't clinical. No one's dying here today." But the thing was, John *was* dying. At least that's how it felt to me, every day, since May a year ago when we'd suddenly learned that his first transplanted kidney was failing.

That's what End Stage Renal Disease (ESRD) means: living with a constant death sentence. Only by managing some type of regular dialysis, severely limiting all fluid intake, sticking to an impossible diet and taking multiple medicines a day can one manage to stay alive. Possibly a patient can get a kidney from a live donor or wait on a list for five to seven years for a deceased one. Combined with John's rare autoimmune disease that had appeared out of nowhere and started the whole scenario ten years earlier, his wasn't much of a life.

When they returned from their beach walk, John flopped facedown across his bed fully dressed and was quickly asleep. Megan showed me the selfie she'd snapped of the two of them, and then I went to bed, too.

The next morning we hugged goodbye, and they left a the outpatient procedure. Only one visitor could stay in the waiting room because of the COVID-19 situation. Megan had recently completed her journey to become John's living donor and was waiting on her transplant committee to meet and, we hoped, grant approval. It was time for me to shift some of my role to her. Along with being his first living donor, I had been his primary caregiver for ten years. I sought the beach, my favorite place, and tried not to think.

More than two hours after Megan's initial text to say they had taken him in for the procedure, I was worried. Megan should have called or texted by now. I lay on my towel, trying to feel nothing but the intense heat. Against my closed eyelids, all I could see was red. I sat up, turned over, and tried again. Again the same bright red. John's initial autoimmune disease had caused internal and pulmonary hemorrhaging; I had seen a lot of blood with him. And this was a heart procedure to check the pulmonary artery.

I reached for my phone and texted Megan. She didn't think it had been enough time and wanted to wait, instead of demanding to know what was going on as I would have done. *This is why I'm letting her do it*, I reminded myself. Nevertheless, I picked up my things and went back to the house.

Megan called within the half hour to say that the procedure was over and she was coming to get me; John would be released soon and we could go home. Everything went well; John's heart and pulmonary artery were fine! He was anxious during the procedure. He had asked for something and was told it wasn't necessary. He had texted Megan and she had tried to advocate for him through the attendant at the desk, and they had given him a small amount of something. The catherization had identified the problem: too much blood pushing through his fistula (the artery grafted to vein creation that was necessary for dialysis), overtaxing his heart and contributing to high blood pressure and fluid problems. This issue could be adjusted and would not be a block for transplant. In fact, with a successful transplant, the fistula would no longer be necessary.

So much history with that fistula! I thought. The first three attempts in Greenville in 2010 had failed. It took a two-phase surgical process at Duke in 2011 to get a successful one. John had much suffering associated with those five surgeries and constantly worried that a careless dialysis technician would "blow an infiltrate" or otherwise damage it. In fact, during his last hospitalization three months ago, the Greenville vascular surgery team had gone in to de-clot and balloon out a narrow part.

John texted me soon after Megan's call to say, "Tell Cousin Betty and thank her for her prayers."

This first cousin of mine, whom I'd not seen in years, had been emailing and texting John almost daily for the past several months. She told me later that John had texted her that morning from the hospital, asking for her prayers. John may not have believed that his own prayers were heard, but he did believe that those of others "better" than himself were. It was another indicator of how afraid he was for the outcome of the procedure.

Then John texted to say he was being released. We hurriedly loaded the car. The drive to downtown would take at least twenty minutes.

We pulled up to the front of the hospital and saw John standing alone on the sidewalk in the strong midday sun of a Charleston July. *Are you kidding me?* I silently screamed. *Why did he walk out alone after a heart cath?* I moved to the back seat and John collapsed in the front. In answer to my questions, he repeated what the doctor had told Megan.

"I'm fine," he said. "Tired. Doctor wouldn't give me anything for anxiety." He pulled his baseball cap over his eyes and leaned the seat back.

"Did they give you instructions?" I prodded.

"Just no heavy lifting."

That was about all we got for the next four hours. It was not the reaction we'd expected for this good outcome. He slept, or pretended to, and pushed away any touches or words I tried to offer.

I recognized this as a PTSD reaction for him; I'd seen it too many times. He pulled deeply inside himself. *To find what? Comfort? Peace? Numbness?* I wondered.

He had not wanted this procedure, or another trip to Charleston.

He was terrified of hospitals, stemming from the countless times he'd been in them experiencing not only near-death occurrences but also extreme pain, panic, and loneliness. He had recounted in *Since John Got*

Sick of listening to a young man's screams in the cubicle next to John in intensive care until he finally died before morning. I had witnessed John's trembling fingers, ragged breathing, irritability, and silence every time he had to seek care—which was frequent.

PTSD, or post-traumatic stress disorder, was even the reason that his federal disability benefit continued after the three-year-post-transplant criteria for End Stage Renal Disease. Testing by a certified administrator had showed severe PTSD. Yet he had never been able to get treatment for it, primarily because of inadequate financial resources. Naturally prone to anxiety and depression, his health crisis at age twenty-six had left him with much greater damage than no kidney function.

In the past ten years, serving not only as mother but also as his advocate, only once did I see the medical community acknowledge his PTSD in any serious way. That diagnosis was listed on every medical record he ever had, and yet there seemed no connection to how present circumstances could be triggering a PTSD reaction. The single occurrence was by a critical care nurse practitioner who had known and treated John on several occasions. At his past March hospitalization, she'd called the psychiatrist (who we'd finally gotten for him within the past year) to say that John needed continuing medication for anxiety, for which she could only prescribe five days. This psychiatrist said, "We're trying not to prescribe those for him." This nurse told her, "He needs them until you deal with the underlying PTSD and psychological issues, or he's never going to get better." She even called a psychiatrist whom she knew specialized in PTSD, but he did not have an appointment for two months and did not take insurance. I was glad for her sole voice of intelligent clarity about a severe underlying condition.

The previous two visits to Charleston over the past six weeks had worn his emotional and overall condition to a thread. Because of his complex history, the transplant team needed to examine every detail. Plus, he'd been hospitalized in Greenville five times in the past seven months. I was with him during those last two transplant exams and watched the gravity of those doctors' expressions, the subtle shake of a head. John saw, too, and we both knew the unspoken: he may not be able to get a transplant. Then there would be nothing but waiting for death.

We had asked that today's procedure be done in Greenville, by the cardiologist who had recently done the "regular" left-side catheterization. Again I was with John at this visit. The cardiologist told me later, "I could see it in both your faces and in John's eyes that he didn't want the procedure."

That doctor had called the Charleston pulmonologist and offered to do it in Greenville but was refused. The transplant team called the shots, they held the life card. Hence another trip, another anxiety-producing experience, on July 22, 2020.

Nonetheless, it was good news. Now all we had to wait to hear from was the Behavioral Health assessment, which possibly was already completed. COVID-19 had delayed the process by months, but in all likelihood, Megan's committee would meet the following day, July 23. How soon would John's case be presented? Could there be time to get surgery scheduled and for Megan to recover before she had to start teaching the second week in August? It was too tight. Being a new teacher and concerned for her job, I understood that she wouldn't delay starting school, and I was afraid John wouldn't last until the Thanksgiving holiday. So many uncertainties.

I wondered if John were thinking these things, too, and more. About the pain and associated trauma that would come with a transplant. He had told the Behavioral Health transplant psychologist that he would not leave the hospital on pain meds. He would be on heavy immunosuppressant drugs. And COVID-19 could be even worse in the fall and winter . . . . Even if we got the "best" news and transplant was scheduled, there was still a rough ride ahead. We knew better this time.

We arrived at John's apartment and he seemed to perk up. His girl-friend Jennifer's car was there. I got out and stood with him as he got his bag out of the rear. He pulled the top closed and reached to hug me.

"I love you," he said.

"Love you, too," I responded.

This wasn't unusual, however normally I was the one to initiate it. Maybe he was feeling sorry for being such a grouch to me on the way home. He hugged his sister, smiled at us, and walked into his place. It was the last time we saw him.

Megan and John, July 21, 2020

2

The In-between Years (2012–2019)

THE KIDNEY TRANSPLANT IN April 2012 had felt miraculous. It had been exactly two years since Wegener's granulomatosis had almost taken John's life and twenty-one months since the rare autoimmune disease had destroyed his kidneys. It took more than a year for him to be approved for a transplant; doctors wanted to make sure the disease was "quiescent." Then a couple of attempts by possible living donors didn't work out, then half-a-year for me to be approved to be John's donor. Besides financial worries for me, the big hold up was a lack of caregivers for either of us. I would be in Durham only a week, but John would need to be there for a month. Yet finally it worked out, with John's father and stepmother helping him and two first cousins staying with me. Many prayers went with us.

After the surgeries, my kidney worked immediately in John's body. (Sometimes patients need dialysis to give the newly transplanted kidneys time to "wake up.") Coming out of the intensive care unit, he looked and felt better than he had in two years. He was full of hope when he left the hospital. And on leaving Durham, he was able to go to the house he would be renting with a longtime friend. I struggled to recuperate and get back to work. Overall, transplant was a success. And no more dialysis!

While Duke had clearly stated, "Transplant is not a cure; it is an alternative to dialysis," I don't think any of us heard that. We had not counted on how hard the immunosuppressant medicines would be on his body. He was susceptible to any germ that came along. A simple cold could turn into an ear infection or bronchitis, requiring an immediate antibiotic. Also he had acquired C. diff, a bad intestinal infection resulting in violent diarrhea and painful cramping, during an earlier hospitalization and it flared several more times over the years.

C. diff usually occurs only in people with compromised immune systems, often elderly patients, and many don't survive it, at least not more than once. John had it six times. The last time (March 2015), he ended up septic in intensive care, yet another time he almost died. After that, he stopped taking antibiotics (which triggered it), preferring to stay sick, unless they were given intravenously for pneumonia or a staph infection. I started researching fecal transplant, which was maybe the only cure for C. diff, and got him on a good probiotic.

Megan offered her services: "Since you gave him a kidney, I'll give him some poop!"

Much of the time we tried to keep things light, because that's who John was. The master of understatement, minimization, and dry wit. He also felt shamed by this condition. While neither the Wegener's nor End Stage Renal Disease was contagious, C. diff definitely was (when it was flaring). He didn't want one more thing to separate him from his friends.

One winter, just after he'd gotten a new job, he developed shingles and could no longer work. Chronic fatigue, for which no one had an explanation, never left him (since 2010). He had difficulty sleeping most nights and took to staying on a sofa instead of a bed. I associated this action with the night terrors he'd had during the early hospitalizations, but all he would say was that he couldn't stop the racing thoughts.

One doctor, whom John trusted, told him it was the pain meds that were sapping his energy. He had remained on two narcotics prescribed from his original hospitalizations. Wanting to do anything to feel more energy, he took himself off these "cold turkey" while refusing any treatment because he was too afraid of hospitals.

He continued to try to find work that he could manage to do—i.e., not standing, not around germs—which eliminated any service industry jobs. He went from data entry with a financial planner to working for an ambulance company to helping a friend flip houses, but nothing lasted very long. He decided that real estate might be a good option, that he could do it on his own timeframe. His father and stepmother paid for real estate school. He studied hard, did well on the state licensure exam, and was pleased to affiliate with a local company. But he did not have the energy or the financial means for all the upfront costs necessary for promotion, nor the ability to be cut-throat enough. While he would have never hesitated to take on someone physically (at least before he got sick) to defend himself or another, he did not have it in him to undercut someone to get a sale.

Yet he was still and always John. I recall a spring weekend when Megan and her family were in town and we were all downtown at the falls. The little girls had stepped across the river on stones, and Jane suddenly lost a flip flop. Instinctively John, agile, lithe, and sure, moved across the river to rescue the escaping shoe. I cherish the memory of him, the least healthy of any of us, "walking on water."

Simultaneously, my life focused on my job and doing all I could to help John. Five of those years required a daily commute to a nearby town. I didn't have time or money for much of anything else. Somewhere along in there, I started writing *Since John Got Sick* and was pleased and surprised when John contributed his part. Writing is something that has always helped me deal with my life. I think maybe it helped him, too.

Another thing I did was to volunteer in the Greenville hospital's intensive care waiting room for four hours on Saturday afternoons. I enjoyed it because it was a tangible and immediate way that I could help families (by interfacing for them with nursing staff, walking them back to see their patients, etc.). I knew the confusion, shock, and fear they were feeling. For those few hours, working with others took me out of my own worry about John. I also worked with a saint who kept reminding me that "God's got this."

In 2016 I made a move to downsize again. I'd been living in a small house for twelve years, but I knew it was time to go even smaller. I couldn't keep up with the yard or the expense. Moving back to the condo complex where I'd lived the first years after the divorce was the right decision. John and his colleague handled my house sale.

My job had also shifted so that I was back working in Greenville with my team, which was a huge benefit. Soon (2018) John got a job as a bank teller and moved into an apartment by himself. Our book was published and life felt a little more manageable. But not for long.

John and niece Jane

3

May 2019

MOTHER'S DAY. HOME NOW, I had been with Megan and her family in Athens, Georgia, the past few days. They were site visiting for jobs, a new school, and a new home. I was ecstatic, and somewhat disbelieving, that they would be this close to Greenville after being too far away for eight years.

I had not heard from John in several days. He had not responded to texts or calls since I'd last seen him Wednesday noon. He had told me then that he needed help with his depression and he seemed desperate.

It had been a bad season. A few months prior, he'd had a significant break up with his first love from high school, and then several weeks ago he had gotten fired from his bank job for missing too much work. I had met him for lunch before I left town and had gotten him to call the local hospital's Behavioral Health intake counselor; he was waiting to hear back. He was out of money and behind on critical bills. I gave him some money, trusted him to get the help he needed, and left to be with my granddaughters while their parents were occupied.

During those few days away, my mind was constantly on my son. Being with happy little girls at the hotel pool, I wondered at the contrast in the lives of my two children. *What had happened? What had gone so wrong with John's life? Was it the idiopathic disease that had almost killed him at age twenty-six?*

Yet John had had difficulties since high school. *Was it because he was only fourteen when his father and I separated and then divorced and life as he knew it shifted drastically, while Megan had been older and got through high school in our home with things basically intact? Was the break-up of our family the first trauma that he never healed from? Was it my family's genetic addiction thread that shadowed him?* I was out of answers, and I was afraid. I didn't know what to do anymore.

John referenced in *Since John Got Sick* his opioid dependence following the initial hospitalizations and his effort in getting off them several years ago. (He had come home from months' long hospital stays in 2010 on a 50 mg Fentanyl patch plus two oral narcotics.) As the years progressed and he was not able to have a successful career like that of his friends, or a lasting long-term relationship, his anxiety and depression deepened. During those years, I rarely saw him sitting on a sofa but always lying down. Chronic fatigue never left him.

What he would not talk about and yet what I thought was his key issue was the post-traumatic stress he'd experienced. It was nearly impossible to get him access to a psychiatrist or counselor because they would not accept Medicare and we did not have the money to pay privately. Only in the past month had he been able to see a psychiatrist because a co-worker of mine appealed to a clinical director at the hospital on John's behalf. John had had one visit and was scheduled to continue.

Around mid-afternoon that Mother's Day, John texted me. "Are you home yet?"

I replied simply, "Yes."

I didn't hear more from him and finally decided I would have to go check on him. I took a friend with me, a man who had more experience with what I felt by this time must be some type of substance abuse. There was no other explanation for his non-responses to me; he always called me if he had a medical need.

John told us he needed to get to a treatment facility. He didn't elaborate and I didn't press; I was only glad that he was willing to get help. He was very depressed and shaky, but I had seen him worse. We called the local center. The response was that they were full and to call back at 8:30 the following morning. Other than his going to the emergency room and claiming he was suicidal, there was nothing else to do. We left and I returned alone with some supper for him. He said he would take himself for treatment the following morning.

He called me that morning to say he was bringing his dog Pippen, a chocolate lab-bull mastiff mix, to me. When he arrived, I could see that he wasn't in any shape to drive. He agreed to let me take him. We were at the door of the center at 8:30, calling on the intercom. Again the response was "we don't have any beds."

Sitting in the car in the parking lot, I had him call a local private facility and listened as he talked with the assessment counselor. Because of his complicated health situation, they would need recent labs. I called his doctor's office and learned that a request had to be made in writing, and then it would take up to three days to get his medical record sent.

Totally frustrated and worried about key work appointments of my own that I was missing, I took John back to my place.

"I'll be back at noon," I said. "Then we're going to the Greer ER. It will be faster. You can get labs and a report done there. Then I can come back and take you to the Greer center. It's right near there."

He called back the intake counselor and she agreed with this plan. They had room and would hold a bed for him.

I left John at the Greer hospital waiting room around 12:30. I had had many years of learning to be responsive to John's needs and to also keep my job, which generally supported us both. I knew he would be safe until I could get back.

Returning to my car, I saw a friend who was a nurse on that campus. She said, "What's wrong?" and I collapsed into tears. There were so few people I could ever confide in, especially about this. My co-workers knew of the seriousness of John's situation and were more than accommodating, but my job was demanding and we all had full plates. I composed myself and drove on to my Greenville downtown office to get ready for a monthly meeting with the Cancer leadership team at three o'clock on the main campus.

Shortly before four o'clock I saw a text come in from John. I read it and abruptly said,

"I have to go. My son is in the ER and they won't let him leave. His kidney is in trouble; creatinine is seven."

I had worked with this group for several years and they knew of John's health issues. They expressed only concern as I hurriedly packed up and left to make the forty-minute drive back to Greer.

When I arrived, I was immediately taken back to see the doctor.

"Have you called Nephrology? Are you sending him to the Greenville hospital?" I asked.

The doctor shook his head and said, "We have been talking to the Duke Transplant Center. They want him there. I'm waiting on a room to open up and then I can call in a report."

Since April 2010 there had been one shock after another with John's health. This one, like the others, came out of nowhere, for both of us. Kidney disease is a "silent killer," and he had had no inkling that anything was amiss, although I wondered later if this could have contributed to his worsening depression the past months.

All I asked was, "Will you call his father? They are supposed to leave for Scotland in three days."

"That's not going to happen," responded the doctor, taking the number with a grim look as he walked away to make the call.

I went in to see John. Coupled with some degree of opioid withdrawal—I was unclear at this point—and severe depression, he'd just received news that we both knew was fatal.

Hours later, Duke still had not called with a bed assignment. I decided to leave to go home to pack, take care of Pip, and make arrangements for her and for work. The Greer doctor had said that since it was getting so late, we could travel to Duke the next morning, but he still needed John to stay in the ER until he could call in a report. My friend who had talked with John the previous day and who lived in Greer offered to pick up John when he could leave and then drive him to my place. But John would have none of it. Finally around 9:30 p.m., he told the doctor he was leaving and called me to come get him. Making my third trip to Greer that day, I picked him up. Since the doctor couldn't complete the information transfer, this meant tomorrow John would have to go through the Duke ER rather than be a direct admit. Nonetheless, I understood; he could have been waiting there until all hours.

In the few hours I'd been home between trips, I had called several people. My friend and neighbor came over and took the initial responsibility for John's dog. My work group quickly worked out a schedule not only to cover my responsibilities but also to come over three times a day to walk Pippen.

It was a somber four-hour drive that Tuesday morning. Cold, shaking, and wrapped in a blanket, John slept a good bit of the way, leaving me to think a million things. My head felt like it was literally spinning. Yesterday I'd thought that he would be admitted to an inpatient program to get help for his depression. Now we were headed to Duke for his—my—failing kidney. *Had I been too old when I donated? Or was it just that it had now been seven years, a "good average" timespan for a donated kidney?*

At one point when he was awake, I said, "I feel like a failure."

To which he responded, "How do you think I feel?"

The wait in the Duke ER was as I'd expected, crowded with patients of every age, race, and condition. John was miserable but did not voice a complaint. He sat in a chair against the gray windows, long legs stretched out in front of him, his cap over his eyes. I got him a blanket. And I went to go to the desk twice to ask how much longer, even though I knew it was pointless.

John could be described as the "strong, silent type." He'd always reminded me of my father in this way, along with his tall, lean stature and winsome grin. I doubt he was always like that with peers, but since the start of his illness he tended to keep most things to himself. He'd told me that none of his friends could identify, and he didn't want to drag them down. I thought this was short-changing his friends, but he did it his way. Always. Even with doctors and clinical staff, especially if they were close to his age as so many were. Often when he would name his pain as an "8," his manner so belied the intensity that it seemed hard to believe him. When it was a "10," he was throwing up and writhing but rarely verbal.

He would tell me, though, and expect me to be his voice. I hated being in that position, even though I could do it well. It started during those initial four months in 2010 when he was so frequently intubated and I literally had to be his voice, providing history and information as best I could. After that, with so much trauma over the years of doctor visits, hospital stays, and procedures, he seemed able only to pull inside himself and endure. He hated being left alone, but the only people he would "let in" were his father, his sister, and me. They weren't readily available. They lived out of town and had other responsibilities.

It was late afternoon when we were finally called back. For the next several hours various teams—Emergency, Hospitalists, Nephrology, Psychiatry—entered the room to examine him, ask questions, run tests, start medications. The Psychiatry group asked John if he were OK with me in the room during their visit, and he said yes. But at one point, I couldn't take it.

"I can't hear this," I said. "I'll be right outside."

I stood in the narrow hallway, my back to the room's glassed-paned door. There were some things a mother doesn't need to know. I really didn't want to hear their probing questions to my adult son. Or the answers he might give.

John was resting more comfortably, waiting to be admitted to a room. I left around 8 p.m. to go check in to the hotel across the street. It was not the one I usually stayed in, but it was within walking distance and I wouldn't have to deal with hospital parking or a hotel shuttle. I was back within the hour. Nothing had changed much. I sat beside his bed, something I'd done hundreds of times.

The gown had slipped off his right shoulder and I could see the famous tattoo, a tidal pool inked in deep aqua. While at the beach, he and a friend had driven across the state line where sixteen-year-olds could get them legally and had charged it on the credit card his father had given him for emergencies.

Thinking about episode reminded of another time–when he nearly died the first time. Easter weekend, eleventh grade. One night at Litchfield Beach, six of them went out in a small boat on the creeks that he loved. They went too far, capsized, hit a riptide, and had to swim all the way back. It was pitch black and 4 a.m. He surprised himself by surviving that one. It was the first of many times he almost died. His long-time friend Emily said she lost count after approximately 732.

It was nearly midnight when John was taken to a room and I went to the hotel. I was back the next morning, this time to John's room. I recognized the unit as the one we'd both occupied after the transplant seven years before.

That morning was bleak in John's room with the blinds drawn and the lights off. He had a bad headache and wanted dark and quiet, which is not the norm for a busy hospital. I tried to run interference as much as possible, but John lost patience with one of the hospitalists who asked the same questions John had already answered a dozen times. John made a couple of forceful retorts, and I thought there was about to be a scene. Then the young hospitalist noticed John's ring and showed him his; they had gone to the same university. He ended up being John's favorite doctor that stay.

John was back on massive doses of steroids and couldn't have anything to eat or drink since he would have a kidney biopsy later in the day. Even that procedure could injure the kidney, but there was no other way to determine the problem. He was refusing dialysis, something he'd been traumatized by and endured for so many months prior to transplant.

I knew he felt he had no reason to live, and I understood that. We had both tried so hard, for nine years, and he'd never been able to make it. What would be different this time?

Megan called; I assumed for an update on John. It was, but she was also in the midst of her own personal crisis. As I was trying to calm her, another call came through from my ex. Telling Megan I would call her back, I answered him.

"It's Dad," I told John. "I'm going to step out."

I updated him on what I knew. "You should come," I said. "You will regret it if you don't."

He was silent and finally said, "All right. I'll be on the way soon."

The drive would take him more than five hours. I went into the darkened room to tell John.

A transplant psychiatrist came in to meet with John at bedside. All his doctors were concerned about the degree of his depression and that he was refusing dialysis, even on a short-term basis. (There was some hope that the failing kidney function could be reversed. More would be revealed after the biopsy.) I left to make my familiar walk to the Duke Chapel.

"Cathedral" would have been a better name. Located centrally on the campus, its spires visible from many angles, it stands as a symbol, pointing educators, doctors, and students to God. It was a beautiful day, unlike the previous day's drear. So many times I had made this walk in the summer of 2010 when John was not expected to survive.

I pulled open the heavy wooden door and entered the massive, vaulted space. No one was there but the attendant in the vestibule. My steps echoed on the stone floor as I walked straight down the center aisle to the altar. Kneeling on the marble steps, I began to pray but all that came out was a sob.

I cried for all the pain of the past years, for John's continued suffering, and mine. This time I prayed only for God's will to be done. Finally, I rose to make the return trip to John's room. As I was leaving, I took a picture of the vibrant stained-glass wall in front of me, knowing I was going to post it on Facebook. I almost never posted anything without checking with John first, but time was different. I said only, "Here in the Duke Chapel again. Praying." I knew that the message would get to those who needed to see it and that they would start praying, too.

Not much had changed in John's room. He was restless, tethered to IV poles. I resumed my seat and we waited.

Almost simultaneously, the nurse let us know that John would be going for the biopsy shortly and his father walked in. He was able to speak to John briefly, and then transport was at the door. They left with John, and the two of us were alone in the room. I told him all that I knew. He was mostly silent.

When John was wheeled back into the room, he was teary and in pain. He had refused any sedative for the procedure. I left him with his father and went to sit in the small waiting room down the hall.

The psychiatrist came looking for me. "Let me get his father, too," I said, and we walked back to the station outside John's room. My ex stepped out and together we listened. He thought that the crux of John's problem was depression–brought on by the break-up and the job loss–and that the unexpected narcotic use was a way to self-medicate. I had watched John struggle to take himself off pain meds a few years ago, and I had thought he would have never used them again. I asked questions and his father listened and nodded. Suddenly I knew he wouldn't be staying.

"When are you going?" I asked.

"I'll have to be getting on the road soon. We leave for the trip in the morning."

"Thank you for coming," I said and turned to walk away. I'm sure he did what he thought he needed to do, but it was hard being the only parent left in a situation as grave as this.

He went into John's room to spend a little time with him and tell him goodbye.

This time I got a coffee and disappeared to the hospital's courtyard. I watched the late-afternoon shadows fall in diagonals from my bench seat. An older woman entertained a toddler. But it was the other woman I focused on and then spoke to.

She was young, Black, heavy, and cradling a tiny baby against her chest. She had a beautiful smile as she replied to my question.

"He's six weeks. He was born early and we were brought here. He has a lot of problems, but we're going home tomorrow!"

Home was rural North Carolina. I thought about the likely severity of conditions that had brought and kept this child here, the probable poor prognosis for his future. Yet this young mother was radiant.

"We're going to do a lot of porch sitting!" she continued. "Lots of family want to love on this boy."

She walked off and again I felt tears sting. I wished that John had more family to surround him, that I did. It seemed like we'd been on our own, both individually and together, for a very long time.

My phone jarred with a text. John probably wondered where I was. But it was from someone I wasn't really close to who was asking, "What is going on with John?"

I assumed he'd seen my post but was surprised he would reach out to me directly.

Before I could respond, he texted again, "I just saw what John put on Facebook."

Quickly I checked John's page. He said that he was at Duke, that his kidney was failing, and that he'd just signed a DNR (Do Not Resuscitate). It read as a goodbye to anyone he cared about.

I hurried back to his room. His father was gone.

"How was it with Dad?" I asked.

He shrugged. "Talked about the trip."

Then I said, "I saw your post."

He faced away.

I tried again.

"I know it feels really dark right now and you are scared. I get it. And I will support you whatever you decide. I am here. And God is with you always. God loves you even more than I do."

No response.

I had said this so many times that I wondered if it seemed only a litany to him. He had told me tearfully several years ago that God did NOT love him. He believed God was punishing him with this unexplained disease that had come out of nowhere.

I sat, through shift change and until the new nurse brought his night meds. I left for the hotel around 9 p.m., telling John to call me anytime and that I'd be back early in the morning.

I'd barely gotten to my room when my phone was ringing. It was one of John's oldest friends calling from Charleston.

He said, "This isn't happening. We got a lot of laughing and living left to do," and proceeded to say that he was going to Greenville to pick up two others, and the three of them would be on the way to Duke the next morning.

I could hardly speak. "Thank you," I managed. Such love from three "brothers" who had been through thick and thin together since grade school.

Then Emily, friend to both John and me, texted. She would drive up day after tomorrow, Friday, stay with me in the hotel, and be there for both of us until Saturday evening. Such gifts.

I slept some that night and was in John's room early, bearing a caramel latte and banana bread for him, along with my own black coffee and blueberry scone. Eating wasn't always important for me but coffee was essential.

John seemed a little better and ate what I'd brought. He'd gotten numerous comments from his Facebook post, as had I from mine. He should hear from the biopsy later today. I told him that his guys were on the way up. He wasn't as excited as I'd hoped. It was almost like he didn't want to face them.

Around midday his friends arrived bringing him lunch and I left them alone, asking that they let me know any news and when they were ready to leave.

I brought supper for John and myself on my return. He'd given up on hospital food years ago and rarely touched a tray. He seemed in better spirits, and we ate and watched television together before I left for the night.

But the next morning he was very depressed again. He'd told his doctors that he was "crying five hours a day." I knew his father had messaged him. I didn't know if John had responded.

Then the attending nephrologist came in to discuss the biopsy results. He drew a picture on the white board to show where there was damage and inflammation. There was some "acute rejection," likely caused by dehydration, but the problem was "chronic rejection." Unlike with an acute infection, this condition could not be reversed. He discussed possible explanations for the cause. There was some chance that in recent weeks John had not taken his anti-rejection meds every morning and night. At John's last visit to the transplant clinic back in the fall, a prescription had been sent incorrectly with only half the dosage for one of his immunosuppressant medicines. The age of my kidney at the time of donation. He still felt that short-term dialysis might help but John was adamant.

Two days earlier, John's first full day as an inpatient, I had put in a request for a social worker or discharge coordinator so that plans could be underway for residential mental health treatment–how we had started on this journey several days ago–when John was released. I had repeated this to his hospitalists but we had heard nothing. It was now close to noon on Friday. I knew not much would get done on a weekend, and that the doctors could decide suddenly to discharge, so I pushed again.

The psychiatrist wanted to keep him as a hospital inpatient because of the degree of his depression, but John would have to start dialysis to justify inpatient status. He still refused. Alternatively, the psychiatrist recommended residential treatment at a facility for depression and co-occurring issues.

Later that night Emily arrived at my hotel room. I was already asleep, having left a key for her at the desk. We talked briefly when she came in after midnight. Then I left her sleeping; she came to John's room midmorning. When she went to get him lunch, I told John that he needed to tell her exactly what was going on. She was a good friend and they had frequent, if not daily, text and phone conversations. She needed to know, and I needed her to know, as someone else to provide him support and accountability. He told me angrily that he was not going to do that, to which I replied that I would then. He screamed at me about confidentiality and told me to "Get out!" followed by, "Why don't you just go to Scotland, too?"

I knew he was angry, hurting, and scared, but I wasn't in the mood either. I let Emily know that I was leaving.

Back in the outside courtyard, I was alone. Even though I was sleeping every night, I was exhausted and hurt and angry myself. I quietly raged for a while—at the situation, at my ex-husband, at John. I had been disappointed and let down, too. The unfairness of everything hit me. *Why couldn't I leave? Why was it always on me?*

Maybe it's in a mother's DNA. Maybe because my mother would never have left me. Maybe because John's situation was too unbelievably terrible. Maybe because I loved him so much. Maybe just God's grace—that I was given the relationship.

Finally I lay on a bench in the sunlight and tried to block out everything.

Around five o'clock Emily let me know that she would be leaving soon. I met her in the round-about and she filled me in. He had been honest with her. She got him talking about career possibilities, finding something he'd really like to do, and she paid for him to start taking a vocational interest test online. While he did that, she had gone to Barnes & Noble and brought him back magazines, puzzles, and a GRE study guide. I was grateful and glad for some positives as I returned to John's room.

He was sleeping. I had watched him struggle to live for so long, against so many odds. It reminded me of his single wrestling season during the winter of his freshman year in high school. He lived off cherry suckers, spitting most of the liquid back into a cup to lose water weight. Unlike his other sports, the focus in wrestling was on two bodies locked in silent struggle for three minutes. From up in the stands I could see the intensity in John's face, the determination and the set of his jaw, as he pinned the senior state champion to the mat. I knew that look.

Then soccer took over, along with high school football, as he used his soccer foot as the place kicker. I was happy to watch him even as a freshman kick the extra point at Greenville High games, my alma mater.

I sat in my spot for over an hour, past dark and suppertime, and then told the nurse I was going to get something to eat and return to the hotel, and to please tell John. That night I turned my phone off.

The next morning I was back in his room early, bearing Starbucks.

He looked at me tearfully. "I thought you'd left," he said.

"Oh, honey! I was here and you were sleeping. And then I asked the nurse to tell you I'd gone for the night! I would not leave you."

He was crying as he whispered, "You're all I have left."

I reminded him that this was not true, but it maybe helped more that I just stroked his hair.

"Want your latte and banana bread?" I asked.

He nodded and tried to sit up.

"It also didn't help that I'm on 1,000 mg of steroids again, too," he said by way of apology.

I had forgotten that. The "roid rage" that can come out of nowhere. And the hunger, which at this point was a good thing.

On Saturday we finally heard from a social worker and had her start on getting him into an inpatient treatment program for depression and help in handling the life he had been dealt. John was ready to leave, as usual—he always wanted to get out—and I knew the doctors wouldn't have much reason to keep him. The next day, Sunday, they aligned with me to keep him at least until Monday when plans could be made, and he reluctantly agreed.

He told them, tears in his eyes, "I just want to see my dog."

But he knew he needed help and that it wasn't easy to get into a facility, as we'd already experienced. I contacted Patient Relations to get a social worker back that day but nothing more happened until Monday. I made a call on my own to a facility in North Carolina but learned that they did not accept Medicare.

Later that day a new attending nephrologist coming on for the week entered John's room. We were glad that it was the doctor that John had seen most in clinic and whom he liked. John asked him more questions and we learned more specifics. He now had 20 percent kidney function; they would increase his immunosuppressant drugs. John asked how long he had on that kidney.

"Months, not years," was the reply. We both quickly commuted that to an eighteen-month average. Eighteen months to live. He was thirty-five.

John wanted to walk. The nurse unhitched him from his lines and we went to the courtyard. He was quiet. At first he was quiet, then he started talking. About his hurt over his father. About the high school relationship that had been rekindled and ended so badly. About things that had happened for him in high school that I had been unaware of.

"I am so sorry that I didn't know. I wish I had been more available to you then," I said. Those two to three years post-divorce had been hard for our family. I was pretty lost myself, and I had also taken a job and was working out of state for most of John's senior year.

By the time we walked back to his room, he seemed more accepting, of everything. I think I witnessed John fully become a man that afternoon.

The next morning whirred with activity, as hospital Monday mornings tend to do. The social worker, who been getting pages from John's team for the past twenty-four hours, had begun her work. She came to the room, and I told her about the private facility that had been willing to accept John a week prior.

She came back to say that the facility would not accept John, even for their Intensive Outpatient Program, because of his kidney situation. The nephrologist was incredulous.

"I'm discharging him to the community! To live alone in his own apartment!" he said.

But they were firm. I guess they perceived it as too much of a liability.

I asked the social worker to try the hospital-based program back home in Greenville that treated depression (although not on a residential basis.). They agreed to accept him in their Partial Hospitalization Program on Wednesday, going 9 a.m. to 2 p.m. Monday through Friday. It wasn't ideal, but it was the best we could do.

Within a few hours the discharge process was completed and John walked out of the hospital with me. We got to my place early evening and John was greeted by his beloved Pip. Then I drove them to his apartment, which had been thoroughly cleaned by a couple of his friends. His guy friends also had gotten his utilities turned back on and paid his rent for both May and June.

The partial hospitalization did not go well; John was too sick. His hemoglobin was so low he barely had the energy to walk to his mailbox. His kidney wasn't making red blood cells (or rather the hormone that produces them), and he had to get two Epogen injections which hit his body hard. Because he missed three days, he was kicked out of the program. His friends talked to him about going to an inpatient program somewhere that they would fund, but John wasn't willing at that point. I didn't have much faith that such a program could be found anyway, after our recent experience. This time it had more to do with his medical condition than with money.

Freshman football

4

November/December 2019

ONE DAY NEAR THANKSGIVING, I met John for lunch at Pete's, a favorite local diner we had frequented his whole life. He had an appointment at the Cancer Institute right after, where he was to have another Epogen infusion. His lack of kidney function caused his hemoglobin to be dangerously low; if it got below seven, he would need a transfusion. While we waited for his sweet tea and my onion rings, he checked his recent lab results on his phone. When he told me his creatinine and GFR numbers (measures of kidney function), I almost slid off the cracked red vinyl bench. I told him I was calling his nephrologist's PA while he went for his infusion. I got him scheduled for an appointment the following week. It was time to start dialysis.

Since leaving Duke last May, John had been continuously sick as his kidney function declined. Many days he couldn't get off the couch except to go to doctors' appointments or take Pippen out. He was seeing a psychiatrist and a psychologist regularly and was working with them to strengthen his commitment to do dialysis when it became absolutely essential. His psychologist nailed his feeling about dialysis when she termed it a "phobia." Yet he wanted to live and knew that he would have to do it until he could get another transplant.

Every day since Duke in May, I knew that he was dying. That thought was constant static in my mind. I knew that he wouldn't be able to work, that he couldn't live off his meager disability income, that it would be too detrimental for him to move back with me in my two-bedroom condo. His father and I had been helping him some for years, but I knew I couldn't do all this. In desperation I reached out by email to my extended family and a few close friends asking for help. They came through for us. While I still supported John significantly, and his father and stepmother paid off his car, it was the fund that kept his rent and utilities paid. I do not know what we would have done without their kindness and generosity.

In August we had moved John to an even smaller apartment in his complex. Megan and my younger granddaughter had come to help. John had collapsed on the sofa halfway through. Four-year-old Jane sat on the floor beside him, coloring and softly singing. It was one of his favorite memories—and mine.

I frequently faced questions from friends concerned that I was too involved in John's life, that I was putting myself at harm physically and financially. I truly did not see how to do it any differently. He was that sick, his health care needs too complex. Also, I was who doctors called if John missed an appointment or needed labs. I was his designated caregiver, his next of kin. Yes, he was an adult, but no one that ill can do it alone.

John's financial existence depended on federal disability, which allowed him to continue to get Medicare in the times he was not in active End Stage Renal Disease. Access to Medicare was far more valuable than the small amount of disability income. Without Medicare he would not have been able to access care or get life-saving immunosuppressant drugs. Because of his minimal income, he was also able to qualify for state Medicaid. Medicaid provides no income but did help significantly with covering what Medicare did not for medications and treatments.

These services—disability, Medicare, Medicaid—required frequent reviews and documentation, which was another task that fell to me. Even though I had a social work background and worked in health care, this was a daunting task. It was equally terrifying; the consequences of losing this assistance would be devastating.

John hated going to the Social Security office. One day as we drove away from one visit where he had just verified to a young man about John's age that he had no other income or assets, he broke down. Sitting in the passenger seat, his head in his hands, he sobbed, "I have nothing."

Being a young adult in his condition had both benefits and drawbacks. Surely his youth and strength contributed to his surviving formidable challenges. Yet the fact that he had not been established in a career, that he hadn't married or made his own family, that he didn't have financial resources to fall back on, left him alone and vulnerable. I had to help.

And he still very much wanted to live a normal life! A career, marriage, and a family were deep values for him. He had worked since he was sixteen. He had gotten through college mostly on scholarships, loans, and part-time jobs. Being attractive for the right person was still important. He hated to take extra steroids because this caused skin breakouts and weight gain. Another method of dialysis–perineal–might be easier for his body, but he would not consider it.

"I'm not having another opening in my body," he stated adamantly, recalling the catheter port he'd had beneath his collarbone for almost two years earlier in his illness.

I understood. I had received the chance to live my life. Whatever I could do to help him live his was my choice. I was grateful for my own good health and strength.

John was able to go to my family's annual Thanksgiving in Atlanta and everyone marveled at how well he looked. He could do that—for short periods of time. He managed to continue to hide how bad he felt from his friends, too, and even to some degree from his father and sister. It was so important to him to maintain some dignity and to try to present as "normal" as possible. But he couldn't hide from me, nor did he seem to choose to, or from anyone physically present with him on a regular basis.

On the way home from Atlanta as I continued to ask him probing questions, he responded angrily to me, "You need to be on anxiety meds!"

He continued to push back hard, and I listened. The next day I called for my own appointment. I knew I drove him crazy with my worry and that he complained to his sister about it. She even told me that was in part why neither she nor or their father ever thought things were as bad as they were, because John said I was overreacting. It was just that I saw his inability to function on a daily basis. I imagine my own PTSD played a part, too; I lived in fear for him every day. But I was sorry I tried so hard to "fix" him; that would have driven me crazy, too.

Getting started on dialysis at an appropriate center still took a couple of weeks. At the first session the first week of December, John got a terrible migraine and had to come off early. (A session usually takes four hours.) His migraines always lasted at least two days. The dialysis sessions never got better, ricocheting his blood pressure and causing the extreme headaches. He was seldom able to do it longer than three hours, and some days not at all, which left him short on sessions. The result was a dangerous buildup of fluids and toxins.

When John had refused dialysis in May 2019, he would as soon have died as go back on it. He had made progress in therapy, even determining that he wanted to pursue a degree in counseling. If he had to do dialysis until he could get another transplant, then he would.

Yet the reality seemed too hard. John could withstand pain. But when I would go by his apartment to check on him, he would be lying on his sofa in the darkened room wearing earplugs and an eye mask. Pippen hadn't been out, and John couldn't move or talk. I observed this situation repeated over and over—while the dialysis center reported noncompliance. Several visits with a neurologist resulted in Botox injections, which helped slightly. This doctor was unable to give him other medications because of his kidney situation, and no one could prescribe pain killers. (The pendulum had swung too far in our state, basically prohibiting anyone but a pain specialist to prescribe a narcotic.) Neither could anyone seem to get his blood pressure under control.

These past years, I had learned so much about kidneys, something I'd never given a thought to before. Besides filtering toxins and certain medications from the blood and releasing those in the urine, they also regulate the body's fluid levels, maintain a balance of salts and minerals (sodium, calcium, phosphorous and potassium), manufacture certain hormones, such as those that make red blood cells, and keep bones strong. A person cannot live without adequate kidney function, and prior to dialysis and then transplantation, kidney failure meant death within a few days.

But we had also learned that neither of the solutions is adequate. Dialysis—whether hemo or perineal—is, in my view, barbaric. And transplant, even when it goes "well," involves life-long, expensive immunosuppressant drugs that make the body susceptible to a multitude of infections. There is also the temporary nature of how long the transplanted organ will last. Neither solution is a cure; there is no easy way. When I gave a kidney at the age of fifty-eight, I simultaneously decided that, should my remaining kidney fail in the future, I would choose hospice over dialysis. I had already asked John's hematologist, who was a friend of mine, "What about hospice?" He had looked surprised and then said, "He's only thirty-five. . .." Yes, and John wanted desperately to live, even though he'd said that he would not see age forty. I couldn't foresee his situation getting any better, and I wanted him to know there was another less painful way.

It all just seemed too hard—for him, and for me to watch.

The first Saturday in December, I went to visit my friend in Charleston. I was exhausted and badly needed a break. I drove down on Saturday, bringing items she'd requested from a local caterer for a party she was having. I got to a Charleston parking lot and called her.

"I don't think I can stay," I said. "John is so sick."

She didn't try to dissuade me, which is why she is my friend, but instead came into town to get the items I'd brought. I called my daughter, too, who encouraged me to remain. I did a bit of Christmas shopping and then went on to my friend's house on the beach. The next day she and her companion took me to lunch, and I talked about John.

"I don't know how this can go on," I said. "I don't know how he is still alive."

"He still has things to teach us," my friend said. I wondered what those could be.

It was the following Saturday morning that I got a call early from John, asking if I could drive him to dialysis, that he couldn't do it himself. I could not remember a time he had asked me to drive him anywhere; in fact, he usually refused if I asked. I hurried to his place, not even showering.

When I arrived, he was having trouble breathing. He had called dialysis to ask if he could come early. I helped him to the car, pulled up in front of the center, and ran in. Before the nurse could come out, two ambulance technicians walked out. (Many patients are transported to and from dialysis by ambulance.)

"Please! Can you come check him?" I implored.

His blood pressure was quite high and his oxygen saturation levels (SATs) low. The EMT's said we should go straight to the emergency room. The nurse said he would call ahead.

John was quickly taken back to the critical care section. Besides his distressing vital signs, one look at his extensive history was always enough to get immediate attention. As soon as I could, I let Megan and their father know and they came.

John was soon admitted and his father stayed with him that night. He was suffering from fluid overload, which compromised his breathing. He was to have a bronchoscopy. Likely dialysis hadn't been pulling off enough fluid—either they didn't have his "dry weight" correct or it was because of the shortened time due to his headaches. His blood pressure remained high, and the bronchoscopy revealed a staph infection in his lungs. Yet he was discharged on the fourth day and was, as always, glad to get home.

The plus about that hospitalization was meeting Jennifer, a lovely young woman who'd been keeping company with John since the Duke crisis last May. John, always private about his personal life, had not told us. They had been friends for years, even going to the same high school and college. I was so grateful to know that he had someone who cared about him and checked on him regularly, as I did. His friend Emily also talked or texted with him frequently, as did his guy friends, his father, and his sister.

The hospital scenario repeated itself two weeks later. This time his dad was in town visiting relatives and he took John to the ER; I met them there. This was an even shorter stay, only two days. Again it was thought to be fluid overload due to inadequate dialysis. His nephrologist was pushing for transplant, and the Charleston program soon called John to schedule the evaluation in March. At last, as December and 2019 ended, there was a date on the calendar. 2020 had to be better.

Thanksgiving 2019

5

March 2020

As JOHN CONTINUED TO struggle with pain, fatigue, and infections, his primary care doctor ordered labs to check for a reoccurrence of Wegener's. His inflammatory markers were elevated. A return of Wegener's and a repeat of his 2010 experience was likely his deepest fear. I tried to get him an appointment with his Duke rheumatologist, whom we credited with saving his life in 2010. However, she was retiring and couldn't see him. One of her partners could see him in June. I searched for a rheumatologist locally.

I managed to get him an appointment with a semi-retired rheumatologist who had just begun practicing part time in our area. I went with John on that Friday. This doctor spent forty-five minutes examining John and reviewing his case before he told us he was not capable of treating him. At least he was honest. He ordered more labs and a chest X-ray and said he would call the Duke rheumatologist. We walked out not saying much. What is there to say when the specialist tells you your case is too complex for him to treat?

John went home and I went back to work. I didn't hear from him that night.

At 9:15 the next morning he called, saying that he couldn't breathe. He wanted me to come and be with him because he was panicking. Knowing his own PTSD anxiety, he often deliberated whether what he was experiencing was only a panic attack. I rushed to his place and sat with him while he tried to breathe and then make it to dialysis at 11. After thirty minutes he said, "I need to go to the hospital," something he hated and feared intensely.

I asked if I shoud call 911 so that he could start getting oxygen immediately, and he said yes. Soon we heard sirens and a team rushed in. Even with the CPAP mask clapped to his face, he wasn't breathing well as they rushed him to the hospital.

I followed in my car, texting two friends on the way. I tried to call Megan who was almost to Tennessee with the girls for spring break. I knew his father was out of the country until the next day. By the time I got parked and through security, John was already in the back. I was taken to a small waiting room.

I knew that room. Chaplains came there to tell you bad news. It also got no phone reception. I waited.

Then one at a time, four friends showed up and found me. One went with me when I was taken back to John's room. Standing outside the glass doors, I could see several people working over him and I could tell he had been intubated. The doctor came out to ask me questions. My friend answered my phone when she saw it was Megan. Peripherally I was watching John as an alarm began going off persistently. The doctor pushed back in; the tube can come loose. I saw John, wild-eyed, flinging about as he struggled to breathe. My friend was screaming into the phone to Megan, "You need to come! Your mother does not need to be doing this alone!"

We were sent back to the little room. My friends sat with me when three doctors came in. John would again be admitted to ICU. This time I insisted they not do chest compressions should that be necessary. John had previously revoked the DNR signed at Duke nearly a year ago and wanted to live, but I could not go along with extreme measures when his future seemed so hopeless. The doctors would call in Palliative Care to discuss options.

I went home for a while but otherwise sat alone in the intensive care waiting room, going back to see John when I was allowed. He was resting comfortably. Two friends and a cousin came to check on me the next day, Sunday. His father and stepmother were coming later that afternoon.

So many hours I had sat similarly. I tried to recall happier moments for John.

John's love was sports, and particularly soccer. I did not enjoy soccer, and it was his father who was the devoted soccer parent. I saw enough to remember John roving the fields for hours and miles, deftly kicking the ball to a teammate poised to put it in the goal. I knew that his athletic training gave him not only the physical stamina but also the mental tenacity to keep pushing through all his difficulties.

When his father arrived, the Palliative Care team met with us. We were on the same page about not wanting extreme measures for John. I wanted John to know his options, that there would be another supportive way when he was too tired of struggling. The team would talk with John when he was off the ventilator.

Again in the waiting room, I asked his father what was his favorite memory of John's soccer life. He thought for a bit and then recounted,

"We were downstate for a tournament. Parents and players ate supper somewhere and then returned to the motel. The boys got together in one room as they often did a night before a tournament. What the parents didn't know was that one of the boys had snuck electric clippers into his bag. As an act of camaraderie and Tomfoolery, they shaved each other's heads and came out of the room with a whoop. They looked like POW's, but they were very pleased with themselves!"

That was who John was, before he got sick.

The following day, Monday, I went back to work. His nurse reported that he'd pulled out the ventilator tube, extubating himself, but said that she would keep him calm and sedated. He was getting dialysis at bedside. One of his friends came to sit silently with him.

When Palliative Care talked with him, he was adamant about wanting to live. He hoped desperately for another transplant. He did agree to having Palliative Care follow him with home visits for medication support.

John was disturbed and crying when I got there at five o'clock. He was frightened and confused. I hoped it was only the medication. I told him Megan was on the way, and I stayed with him until she arrived. His father was coming back at nine to stay the night.

At work the next day, I got a call that John was to be discharged. I hurried to the hospital, knowing that we needed a good plan for going forward. During that process, I learned that John had been out with friends the Friday night before this episode and had a few drinks, and I was furious.

"You cannot do this," I screamed at him in his ICU room, with his father, sister, stepmother, and nurse practitioner present.

I didn't think he was ready to be released, but there was nothing I could do. I grabbed my pocketbook and ran out of the ICU, telling his father he could deal with it all.

From John's view he had moderated his habits and had just wanted a night out with his friends and to be "normal." However, anything at all in his situation was dangerous, as this proved. Even the liquid itself. He could only have 1.5 liters of any fluid—less than a two-liter bottle of Coke—*total* in the timeframe between dialysis sessions. After my outburst, the Critical

Care nurse practitioner, who was also his friend, spelled it out for him, too. His father and sister committed to taking more responsibility for following up with him. His father was to call him every day at 9 a.m. to make sure he was up and going to dialysis. Everyone knew I was stressed to my limit.

After I left, our young friend Emily checked on me and insisted I go for a massage that she'd scheduled for me. There I told the masseuse about my left arm which I'd hurt when I'd fallen at John's one night the previous week. She insisted that I get it checked, so my next stop was urgent care. My arm was indeed broken. I had been so focused on John that I'd been unaware.

Simultaneously that second week in March, COVID-19 became the most important word in the world. John was scooted out of the hospital, partly for his own safety and also to make room for what was to be an onslaught. Megan got word that she would be teaching remotely, and everyone began to figure out how to deal with quarantine.

And the most immunocompromised patients continued to go to community rooms of dialysis chairs in order to stay alive.

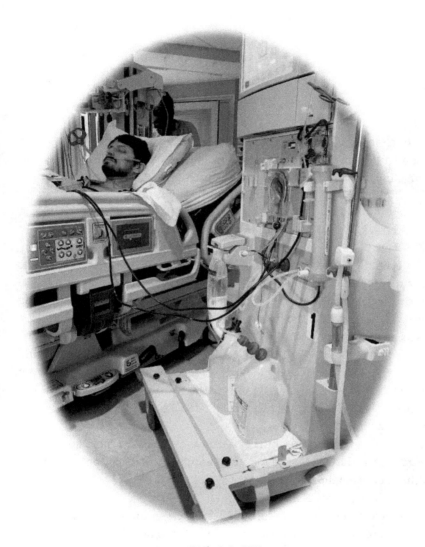

Dialysis in ICU

6

April 2020

I GOT TO JOHN's place before the ambulance. It was just after midnight on a Sunday. I let myself in and found him sitting on his sofa, head down and struggling for a breath, Pippen pacing nearby.

"EMS is on the way," I said. "I hear the sirens now."

He nodded and I hurried back out, to direct them to the apartment. The firetruck arrived first, stopping on the street. I waved them down.

"Hurry!"

Then the ambulance pulled into the driveway. As I turned toward the apartment, I saw that John had already walked out, desperate to get to the needed oxygen. Soon they had clapped a mask on him and were getting him onto a stretcher. The female attendant turned to me with questions. Staccato-like, I responded.

"He just called me. Said he couldn't breathe. He's on dialysis, End Stage Renal Disease. He gets fluid overloaded. Blood pressure has been out of control for weeks. He was confused earlier, and aware of it. I talked to three doctors this afternoon! They said it could be a reaction to something and to wait it out. . .."

Standing at the back of the ambulance as she asked more questions, I heard John inside uttering sounds and motioning. She saw, too, and barked at the attendant adjusting the mask.

"He's saying MORE, MORE!"

Quickly the technician turned up the oxygen full force and John collapsed backward onto the stretcher, finally able to breathe.

"Do you think it could be COVID?" I asked her as she started to close the rear door.

"No," she said. "I think it's his underlying condition. The hospital will call you," then "Go!" to the driver, and the door slammed.

I stared at the red taillights racing from me as the siren screamed again.

John was in COVID-19 isolation for about a day, but I didn't know it at the time. There was minimal communication with the hospital as COVID-19 hit. I knew he was immediately intubated—maybe even in the ambulance. Second time in two months. I can't remember how many times overall in the last ten years. When he is intubated, he is unaware of anything, until they start lowering the sedation. Then he pulls the tube from his mouth and throat. I guess it's instinctive to him.

I did get a call then, to tell me he that he self-extubated, and co-workers heard "mama bear" come out as I unloaded on the pulmonary resident. John was to have surgical repair on his fistula the following day, where he would have to be intubated *again*.

"You *knew* he would try to do this! The nurse practitioner put it in the notes last night!" I seethed. I demanded that he have his attending physician call me.

Apparently they had begun lowering his sedation per protocol, and John was so quick—and still so strong—that he managed to heave his whole upper body forward to reach his hands, strapped down at the wrists, to jerk out the tube before the ICU nurse could get to the bed to stop him. Then he was struggling to breathe and crying. . .. I could visualize the scene as it was reported to me. I knew he was scared and wanted me to be there, and I couldn't be. My one comfort in his being in the hospital alone had been that that he was unconscious; now that had been taken away from both of us. Of course I knew that he would have to be extubated—the breathing tube removed sometime, but not prior to the next day's surgery and hopefully not until just prior to him being discharged to a floor room or even home.

April was John's fifth emergency hospitalization in as many months. December had two, January none, February one, March one, and now April. Each time was worse.

The problems were basically the same each of these five times. In March I had gone a bit berserk, screaming at everyone in his ICU room. Yes, he was fluid overloaded. Yes, he was not getting adequate dialysis. Yes, his blood pressure was out of control. This time there was heart involvement. So why hadn't Cardiology been called in? WHY can't any doctor get his blood pressure under control? And WHAT was Nephrology doing? Could Psychiatry not give him something to control the anxiety during dialysis? What about something for pain to make the migraines bearable? Such a catch-22.

Unlike the March hospitalization, this April crisis was different. John had been doing everything "right;" I checked. He had not missed dialysis time. He'd been measuring his liquid. Vascular Surgery had altered his fistula. This time Cardiology was to follow him, and a heart catheterization was to be scheduled. All I could think to focus on next was his diet. I located a source affiliated with the hospital that could prepare renal diet meals and ordered them.

On his fifth day of this ICU stay, with the help of a nurse, John called me via FaceTime. When I answered, he was crying.

"What is it?" I demanded.

"I didn't think I'd ever see you again," he choked out, his voice still weak from the intubation, another surgery, and surviving yet another time.

I picked him up the next day at the hospital's front door and drove him to his home where Pippen, all eighty-five pounds of tail-wagging love, was waiting. It was around noon on Friday, and he'd seen no one but hospital staff since the previous Sunday at midnight. We stopped on the way to pick up a week's supply of the renal diet meals.

One significant change that occurred after the April hospitalization was that John started training to do home hemodialysis. The social worker at his dialysis center had been trying to talk him into this relatively new option. She thought, rightly, that it would help him feel more in control of his situation. John had been too anxious to do it, but with COVID-19 involvement, he decided to try.

He went for one-on-one training with a dialysis nurse every day for several weeks. He liked this nurse and established a relationship with him. After a few weeks, the nurse monitored the set-up of the dialysis machine in John's second bedroom. John gave the bed to a neighbor, bought utility shelves for all the necessary supplies, and was pleased when his father and stepmother sent him a special reclining chair. A small refrigerator sat beside his chair so that he could store necessary substances and the blood samples he had to capture. The nurse stayed with John in his apartment daily until John felt confident on his own and then stopped by regularly to check on him or to bring supplies. John learned to make a "buttonhole," the two holes in his fistula (which flowed with arterial blood). A bad stick meant blood spray everywhere. But he did it. It did give him more control and some confidence as he mastered a delicate procedure and kept daily logs of things I didn't understand.

Two other good things happened in April. Jennifer was working remotely and came over as much as she safely could (a couple of times she'd been exposed to COVID-19 and wouldn't risk it). John hated being alone and the forced isolation was awful. Most days she sat with him while he "ran" on dialysis. She had helped him purchase the small refrigerator, and together they set up the room and put up the shelves.

"When it was done," she told me, "We high-fived each other and John said, 'And we didn't even kill each other!'"

John also started a small garden plot outside his apartment with Jennifer's help. He grew beautiful vegetables and sent us pictures. Each morning in his father's call or text, the garden was the topic. When Megan's girlfriends asked about her conversations with John about her possible donation, she, too, replied, "We talk in vegetables."

That was John, holding most of us at bay.

Another positive about the home hemodialysis was that it was two-and-a-half hours five days a week, rather than the four hours for three days that were intolerable for him. The shorter, more frequent times did not cause such extremes in fluid levels in his body, which helped with his blood pressure. The migraines stopped. He finally saw Cardiology who put him on five medications, and his blood pressure began to stabilize. His heart catheterization was scheduled.

Every Sunday night John counted out his pills for the large fourteen-dose container that stayed on his coffee table. Bottles of those that had to be taken more than morning or evening, or at otherwise irregular intervals, lined the table as well, beside the blood pressure cuff and notebook to log his numbers several times a day. He somehow managed it all, plus dialysis.

During this time, I, too, limited my exposure to John, out of caution. He would not have survived COVID-19. The biggest healthcare crisis in our lifetime was hitting the industry I'd worked in for nearly thirty years. While marketing was non-essential, communication was critical and some roles shifted. I was grateful to be called in onsite. People were being laid off left and right, and I needed my job.

A high point was working with an ER doctor who championed the patient experience and fostered a project to get iPads to nursing units so that patients could communicate by FaceTime with their families. One such occasion, which we filmed for social media, was with a patient, who desperately needed a liver transplant, and her husband. I felt a part of their story when she was able to be flown to another state to receive a liver.

Another positive experience was coordinating with the Rapid Innovations Taskforce and watching as these amazing doctors, researchers, and entrepreneurs developed new life-saving devices, creative manufacturing and supply sources, and innovative uses of medications that had previously been used only to treat cancer.

I also had the opportunity to visit briefly a young man about John's age in the ICU where John had been so recently. We were hoping to use the iPad with this patient, but he was suddenly not stable. His nurse stepped in quickly and shooed me out. I was grateful to see her attentiveness and care, and to witness that she and others were the family to our patients when we relatives could not be present.

Home hemodialysis

7

May 2020

JOHN ENDED THE ZOOM call with the transplant nephrologist. Seated beside him on his sofa, I breathed and turned to look at him.

"That's the most hope I've felt in over a year."

He nodded. "Me, too."

John had been scheduled to visit him in Charleston in March but all transplant visits had been stopped due to COVID-19. John's was one of the first to be rescheduled remotely. This doctor had reviewed all his records and had spoken with his Greenville nephrologist. More than that, he had had his own experience with a life-threatening illness, and he understood personally the patient perspective. He was able to reflect many of John's feelings, which helped John verbalize more. He completely understood John's wish not to go back to Duke, despite the clinical excellence he'd received there.

"It's even the smell when I walk in the building," John said.

The doctor smiled and nodded.

"Let's get this going then," he said.

The doctor was happy to hear that John's sister had already started the Living Donor process. He commented to me, "Your kidney was a 4:6 match. His sister's should be a perfect 6:6! Let's see if we can make this one last thirty years!"

He heard my concern that we might miss Megan's window; she was a teacher and the summer would be the time she could do it.

He said, "I will make this a priority. And as soon as I get off this call, I will contact the director of the Living Donor program and make sure she is fast-tracked."

He did what he said.

John and I both were almost teary when the call ended. It was a Friday afternoon in early May, and the start of Mother's Day weekend. I was driving to Athens the next day for my granddaughter's birthday. I could hardly wait to tell Megan this positive news.

The day after the phone call I was in Athens, sitting outside with Megan's family and in-laws for the COVID-necessitated drive-by birthday party for our nine-year-old. I shared happily about the call with the transplant nephrologist and watched it fizzle like a dud firecracker. It was obvious that Megan wasn't ready yet to make this commitment (even though she had talked about it for years and it was "understood" that she would be John's next donor), that her husband wasn't fully onboard, and that his parents did not know that Megan had started the Living Donor process. Obviously it wasn't the most appropriate time and place, but John was running out of time. The day ended awkwardly and I drove back home.

A new problem that emerged for John in May was gout, which he had not experienced with the regular hemodialysis. He exchanged migraines for gout.

Uric acid crystals accumulated in the joints caused sudden intense pain, warmth, and swelling. (Removing uric acid is another thing kidneys do.) The medication prescribed by the nephrologists as preventative could not be taken when an attack was active—because it would make it worse—and John's gout was almost constant from when it first started. He saw another local rheumatologist and she prescribed medication, but it could only be used in minimal amounts because of his limited kidney function. John suffered with it in his wrists, knees, ankles, and feet. Jennifer reported that many days she would have to help him walk from his sofa to his dialysis chair.

Of course I was aware of this and advocated for him, but without much success. I had had gout attacks shortly after donating the kidney, and the pain was excruciating. When it happened to me, I was given a steroid shot, pain meds, and preventative colchicine. John had nothing but Tylenol, which was the same as nothing for him.

Pain had been an issue since the onset of his original disease, Wegener's granulomatosis. Wegener's, or GPA, is an extremely painful and rare disease. From his initial four-month hospitalization and a couple of years after, he was on heavy prescription opioids. He had taken himself off these, until the problem had surfaced again briefly in 2019. Along with his history, the medical community's restrictive stance on prescription opioids, which had developed over the past few years, made it virtually impossible to get him any help for pain. The neurologist had given him a limited amount of hydrocodone for the migraines. Even Palliative Care could not prescribe; the nurse practitioner was afraid she would lose her license. His primary care provider referred him to the Pain Clinic. After two months, John had never gotten a call for an appointment.

The critical care nurse who knew him well told me in most non-technical terms, "His pain receptors are blown." She frequently communicated this to the doctors who were unfamiliar with him and who were uncomfortable giving him doses outside of the usual protocol. He had been on so much heavy pain medication and for so long during the 2010 hospitalization that his tolerance never normalized. In the ER when he asked for Dilaudid, staff immediately thought "druggie." He would then have to endure hours of pain while they tried their protocols and watched them have no effect. No way was this his "fault." Nor was it the fault of doctors at Duke trying to save his life. But perhaps it is the fault of medical professionals and state laws that suddenly curtailed prescription narcotics.

Even his primary care doctor, who responded to multiple calls or texts, sometimes daily, once told John to "take Advil and push fluids," neither of which he could do. Such a compromised patient like John (and too many others, I imagine) with so many multi-faceted problems and such a string of specialists made the whole painful mess nearly impossible.

I once asked this provider, who was about John's age, if John was his most critical patient.

"YES!" he responded. "I lose more sleep over him than any patient I've ever met. His threshold for a little sick to incredibly sick is almost non-existent."

Another of my favorite texts from this doctor came when I was trying to decide if an ER visit was necessary: "He doesn't cry wolf. I would go."

The garden

8

June /July 2020

MEGAN HAD HER DONOR evaluation in Charleston early June and I met her there. We stayed at my friend's the night before. I wanted to be there for Megan even though she didn't need me. Whereas John wanted me to be a part of everything, Megan did it all herself and I spent much of the day in waiting rooms or sitting beside the human-sized teal-patinaed frog in the courtyard. Maybe she thought I would try to influence her. She had already done several steps of the process while in Athens. This was a two-day evaluation with various doctors and other professionals. I had been through these days before with John, and for myself. I had hoped to see John's transplant coordinator, whom we'd not experienced to be very help-ful, but she was working remotely. I left a message at the desk for her to contact me.

As we were leaving the hospital Friday afternoon and Megan was telling me about her day, John's coordinator called. She was unaware that John's labs had already been sent and she seemed not to have the sense of urgency that I perceived to be necessary. I reiterated Megan's time window, and the coordinator said, "It can be done later."

Suddenly I was crying. When she probed, I whispered, "I don't think he can live that long."

She responded flatly, "Why? He's on dialysis, isn't he?"

I sincerely wanted her to have to experience dialysis even for one day.

I told her I would be calling the transplant nephrologist and ended the call.

I hung up to see Megan's fury. "I was just telling you that they said I needed TIME to process this, and all you're doing is pushing!"

I couldn't argue although I did try to apologize. I knew she had much to consider, that much was at stake for her. It's a huge ask. I had gone through my own doubts and questions when I had decided to donate. Yet I couldn't stop thinking that John was out of time.

We got to my friend's who wanted to hear about everything. All I could do was hug her, COVID or no COVID, and choke back a sob. Telling her I was going to the beach and saying goodbye to Megan, I escaped to my place where the sand held my cries. When I returned to the house, I told my friend what had happened.

"I told God on the beach that if he didn't want me to keep fighting for John, he shouldn't have made me his mother," I said.

I didn't know why I felt so strongly that John was dying; no one else seemed to think this or want to believe me. Maybe it was just that I was so close to him, physically and emotionally, and because I lived in the health care arena and understood better how complicated, complex, and fragile his existence was. Jennifer, his dialysis nurse, and I were the only ones ever physically with him. John should have died in 2010, and he was spared. Every day was a bonus. I never lost sight of that.

As I got in the car to drive home, Megan called and we were able to talk it out. Then John texted to say the transplant coordinator had just called him to say she had scheduled an appointment for him in Charleston on Tuesday. I guess my breakdown had not been in vain. I'd be heading back to Charleston, this time with John, in three days.

That visit, on June 9, was John's extensive evaluation with the transplant surgeon and to get scans and blood draws. The surgeon was concerned about the multiple complications John had had post-surgery with the first transplant, which we'd never exactly heard specified, and also about his pulmonary hypertension. He was a complex patient and they were looking under every rock.

Exhausted, John slept all the way home. I texted with his dialysis nurse, who would check on him the next morning. The nurse commented on some short-term memory loss that he'd noticed and said that John was still "medically fragile."

I found myself continuously adjusting my hopes and dreams for John. I had told the surgeon, "He was never sick!" something that still seemed to baffle me. Yet something the surgeon said had opened another thought line. Something about conditions probably always being present in his body. I didn't get all of what he said; I couldn't comprehend it fully. The hope I had, though, was that God knew from the beginning that John would have all these serious health concerns and yet struggle through. That I would be a participant. That it must be for some purpose, have some meaning.

I was exhausted, worried, and overwhelmed. Whether they would accept him, when they would decide. I wondered at the why of it all, the *duration*. It was as if I were being carried forward on a wave of energy not of my own making or within my control.

John let me know two days later that a Charleston hematologist had called him and then cleared him. He had also been cleared by Infectious Disease. Then appointments were scheduled with Pulmonology and Behavioral Health in Charleston on July 7.

Since May, I had been pushing to get fundraising started and a webpage set up. We had done major fundraising prior to the 2012 transplant and now there was little time. I wanted to set up a trust for John that would continue when I could no longer work or help him financially. I met with an attorney who specialized in creating those for Medicaid-assisted people. COVID-19 caused delays in this process, too, and there was still nothing in hand at the end of June.

But Jennifer was creating a website, teamGREENE.org. She was also doing a surprise video for John, to show him how much his friends and family cared about him. John was hoping to go to the lake to meet up with some of them for the July Fourth weekend but didn't know if he'd be able, especially with the Charleston appointments upcoming on July 7. The gout attacks continued to be awful. His dialysis nurse told him, "Go. It will do you good."

He made it. One of his friends sent me a picture of John on the boat. His skinny, pale, shorts-clad legs were covered with a towel, and a bottle of sunscreen and one of water were beside him. He had a smile on his face.

On Monday, John got his dialysis done by 2 p.m. and we were able to leave for Charleston. The next morning, again at my friend's, he came into my room and he was crying.

"What is it?!"

"Look at this," he said and handed me his phone.

It was the video Jennifer had created with messages of love and support from many of his friends and family. I hugged him, tears in my eyes, and we left for another day of appointments.

The first was with the pulmonologist, to whom John had been referred by the transplant surgeon for pulmonary hypertension. This doctor asked more questions than anyone else previously. Apparently he didn't want to read the medical record or didn't trust it, so he had John recount his entire history since 2010, and he typed all this into his notes. His visit summary listed forty-two past or present diagnoses. At this time, John was on twenty-nine prescription medications. He ordered an echocardiogram for John later that day, plus a right-sided heart catheterization to be scheduled to rule out high-output heart failure. He noted that John's fistula was aneurysmal and ordered a fistula study be done along with the cath. His grave manner, with the subtle shake of his head, communicated words he did not say. I knew that John and I were both hearing: *He may not be approved for transplant. He may be too sick.* I was again amazed at how critically complex his condition was. I marveled that John could still manage to live.

It was at this point that I requested that this heart cath be done in Greenville by the excellent cardiologist who had done the left-sided one a month ago. This pulmonologist seemed to think that would not be an acceptable alternative, but he agreed to talk to the cardiologist whom John was already scheduled to see the following day. He seemed irritated by my request and showed no concern for timeliness, convenience, or patient preference.

John was scheduled to meet with the Behavioral Health psychologist at 1 p.m. After lunch we located the building. It was pouring rain when entered the facility, only to learn from the security guard that all staff were working remotely. We went back to the car and John searched his phone for a possible number to call. Then his phone rang; it was the psychologist. His appointment had been rescheduled the previous afternoon to an online visit and he had not seen the email. So the appointment occurred in the front seat of my car.

The psychologist asked John if he were OK with me being present and he said yes. I don't what other choice he had—it was raining heavily and I had nowhere else to go. John certainly didn't want to reschedule it.

For the next 90-plus minutes, I listened as John responded to questions and talked about his 20-year past with anxiety, depression, PTSD, and addiction to pain meds. It was grueling. I was exhausted when it concluded and amazed at his strength to face honestly those things in his past. He still needed to re-send her the online tests and questionnaires that he'd completed, and that she had not received. I knew Jennifer would make sure those got sent that night. I asked the psychologist about her timeframe, and she said she would have her report done by the end of the weekend. (This was Tuesday.) John also needed to get another blood sample sent from a local lab.

Then we had to go back to the hospital for John to get the echocardiogram, which took longer than I'd expected. Finally we were on the way home.

Two days later, a Thursday, was a very bad day. John overslept and was confused when Jennifer finally got him to come to the door close to noon. She let me know, and I called the dialysis nurse to ask him to please check on John. The nurse had them both put on masks, and John immediately began having a reaction with his eyes stinging and tearing. He had badly hurt his knee the previous Saturday at the lake, and along with the gout, could barely walk. But he said he was OK to start dialysis. The nurse left and Jennifer stayed.

Then Jennifer called me again. Arterial blood spray was all over John, the chair, and the wall, and the nurse Doug was on his way back. Doug tested him for Covid-19 and thought I should take him to urgent care to see about his eyes and his knee, but John wanted to wait and see. Jennifer told me later that he'd broken down with her that night about how bad he felt. When she was leaving, he said, "You should take a key."

The following Tuesday, John decided to go to urgent care and asked me to take him. He couldn't put weight on this knee, and Jennifer was helping him walk from the sofa to the dialysis chair. My car was in the shop; I said I would be there as soon as I could get it at five o'clock.

Several weeks before, a mouse had gotten into my car and died. It had been quite an ordeal to get the creature out, requiring hours of labor, disassembly, and new parts. Then suddenly two days ago, my air bag warning light had gone off. I had left my car that morning with the mechanic, saying that I had to have it back by five p.m. However, when I called at four to check on it, I learned that it was in pieces in the shop. The cause was still undiagnosed, and it was not possible to get it back together that day.

"I have to get my son to urgent care!" I protested. "And I NEED my car!"

Finally the attendant suggested that someone would take me to rent a car. The driver picked me up at 5 p.m. and soon I walked in the rental agency to get a car. The driver waited. I handed my driver's license to the employee. After looking at it, he said, "Do you have another one?"

I stared at him. "What are you talking about?"

"Ma'am, this one expired the first of this month."

Obviously being aware that my driver's license needed renewing had not crossed my mind during these times. There was nothing he could do to help me.

I walked back out, got in the car with the driver, and said, "Well, you're stuck with me." He looked nervous.

I considered options and then told the driver, "Take me to my son's. And pick me up at my place at 8:15 in the morning. And get my car back TOMORROW, no matter what."

Jennifer wanted to take John but he said, "Let her do it. She knows how to handle things."

I drove John's car and when we got to urgent care, I insisted on being allowed to go back with him. Then the wait inside the room was interminable. When the doctor finally finished his supper break—he told us this—and came in, I was thoroughly out of patience and John just wanted to leave. This doctor began trying to dissect the ten-year history of all John's conditions, to which I said, "Are you going to give him a steroid shot or not? Otherwise, we just need to go." He walked out huffily and a nurse came in.

I recognized her as one of the ER nurses we had seen before. I made the connection for them since usually she'd seen him prone and struggling for breath. She was amazed when she learned that he was doing home hemodialysis by himself.

"You should just go ahead and become a doctor!" she said.

John smiled.

Her comment was definitely the best thing about that day.

Maybe it was that the recent conversation with the Charleston psychologist was still in my mind, but something triggered in my gut. Something else was wrong. The oversleeping lately, the confusion, even the eyes burning. Jennifer also said that John's car had been moved from where it was between the time she'd left the night before at 11:30 and when she'd come back that morning. When I asked John specifically about this, he told me that he'd gone to the local QT to get dip. (He was still struggling with recently quitting smoking.)

I continued to limit contact with John the next several days, trusting his dialysis nurse and Jennifer to be there for him, along with God and John's angels.

I sought out a FAVOR coach and talked to her. FAVOR—Faces and Voices of Recovery—had a strong peer-based community in our area. I learned from her that there was also a home-based program run by a nurse for those chronically ill. I filed this information away. John had turned me down so many times about FAVOR options, continuing to say that he didn't have a problem anymore and didn't need any help. My plan was to wait for the outcome of the Charleston Behavioral Health evaluation and present this as a last option if transplant could not go forward at this time. As we'd already learned, there was no help available (other than the sporadic counseling he was receiving) prior to transplant. All I knew to do was to push on through for transplant, regardless.

John learned that the pulmonologist was insisting that the right-sided heart cath had to be done in Charleston by his guy; it was scheduled for the following Wednesday, July 22.

A few days after the urgent care trip, John again did not wake or start dialysis until after 3 p.m. when Jennifer went to check on him. Pippen had not been out.

She let me know and I texted John. When he responded, I asked point-blank, "What is really going on?"

He responded with, "I'm f*****g depressed!" and expanded on how miserable he was.

I knew this to be true and apologized for pressing, saying, "I don't want to make it worse." I offered again to try to get him help, but he gave no response. I thought it was a PTSD episode that took him to dark places. I continued to pray. The next day he was better and called to apologize to me.

He spent time with Jennifer that weekend. They went out to eat and even went over to a friend's house briefly. I gave thanks for Jennifer every day, that God had put her in John's life. She wanted nothing more than to love and be with him. He trusted her, as much as he ever trusted anyone. She had the fundraising site almost ready to launch, and I was to sign papers on Monday at the attorney's office for the trust. And Megan was coming Tuesday to drive us to Charleston.

After a long day Monday, I was packing for the trip and already undressed when John texted me around 8:30 p.m. He had run out of gas two blocks from his apartment, had no money, and needed me to come. And I really didn't want to. I was just so tired.

Nevertheless, I picked him up, took him to the gas station, and gave him $20 for gas. I grilled him about extra money I'd just given him Saturday, and he was angry with me. I let him out at his car, literally in sight of his apartment, and waited, watching in the rearview mirror as he poured gas into his tank. He motioned me on. I knew he hated having to call on me or need me so much. I waved and drove off.

He knew I was wearing out.

Megan and I would pick him up the next day for the last Charleston trip and procedure on July 22.

Fourth of July outing

9

July 23, 2020

I WOKE THE MORNING after John's last heart catherization, feeling calm for the first time in many days. I was grateful that I could just go to work that day and do my job. The transplant evaluation process was done; now we were just waiting to hear the verdict. We didn't know what that would be.

That day three of us were handing out COVID-19 t-shirts to staff from 11 a.m. to 1 p.m. in the main hospital cafeteria. As normal, I didn't text John that morning, leaving that to his father and Jennifer.

It was noon when Jennifer called. She always texted. I answered to hear her crying hysterically.

"John is cold and non-responsive!"

"Call 911—I'm on the way!"

"I already did," she said.

Turning to my two co-workers, I relayed her message and said that I had to leave.

One immediately said, "Do you want me to go with you?"

I realized that I did and looked to the other for affirmation that she would be OK alone.

"Go!" she said.

We hurried to my car and I drove the less than ten minutes to John's apartment. I could not have picked a better person than this co-worker to be with me. Besides having known her for twenty-five years, she was a rock of calm and even a nurse. I don't remember talking on the way but only thinking, *If the ambulances are still there when I get there, he will be gone.*

We pulled up to the driveway. The street was partly blocked with emergency vehicles.

"You go," she said. "I'll park."

I headed straight to Jennifer on the sidewalk, who was holding Pippen on her leash and sobbing, "He's dead! I thought they were going to help him, not come tell me he's DEAD!"

An officer walked up to me and I said, "I'm his mother."

"You can't go in right now. Not until after the coroner gets here."

"I don't want to," I said, and turned my focus to Jennifer sitting on the curb dissolved in tears.

Kneeling beside her, I said, "Call your mother."

I felt guiltily grateful that Jennifer had taken this bullet for me. For years, my constant prayer was that I not be the one to find John dead. That was answered at Jennifer's expense. She had brought her blonde light into John's darkness.

My friend took Pippen's leash. Then I called Emily, who said she would be on her way immediately. Next I called John's dialysis nurse who had been such an integral part of our little team the past months; he came quickly. Also a man of few words, he commented, "John fought the darkness, but there was still a lot of light in him."

Then I knew I had to call John's father and Megan.

My ex and I didn't talk much. Usually it was texts and then only during a crisis.

I wondered, *How do you tell someone his son is dead?*

He answered and I said, "This is the call you've never wanted to get."

Immediately he broke down. "No, Allison, no. . .!"

Suddenly I had a vivid memory of the time I'd called to tell him I was pregnant with Megan. We had been married seven years and it didn't seem like it would ever happen. He had cried then, too.

I asked if he were alone and he said his wife was there. He would let me know when they were on the way.

Then I tried to figure out how to tell Megan. I knew that her husband was in a seminar that day and that she would be home alone with the little girls. Only eighteen hours ago, she had been in this very driveway. I tried calling and texting her husband several times and he never picked up. Finally I called her mother-in-law in Atlanta, asking if she would go to Athens to tell Megan and stay with the girls.

I texted John's primary care doctor who called quickly; I passed the phone to an EMT. I had already told the EMS team of John's complicated health conditions.

Emily and her husband arrived, and he took Pippen home with him. Jennifer's parents got there. My co-worker had let our work group know. I called my minister friend and he came.

Then Megan called, sobbing. Her husband had gotten my message and called her. She was standing in her backyard where the girls couldn't hear her. Her husband came home soon and then they, too, were on the way.

Time had no meaning as we stood on the black asphalt driveway, waiting. The sense I had standing there waiting was finality. This was not yet another time when John teetered over the edge of death. I didn't have to desperately seek help for him, plead with his father and sister to come, beg God for his life. It was over. Maybe that's why I didn't cry then.

The first officer on the scene took Jennifer aside. I could see her shaking her head. Then the two of them approached Emily and me, and he asked about drug use. Jennifer had never seen John have anything but alcohol. Emily and I knew more. Both of us nodded.

"In the past," I said. "Prescription meds."

Emily added, "Cocaine in college."

I wondered if they asked these questions of any young person who died suddenly.

As we waited, I posted a photo on social media that I had of John asleep on his sofa with Pippen beside him, along with the message, "Our beautiful son, brother, uncle, and friend left this world today. . .."

Finally the coroner came to talk to us, along with a female detective. These two young women could not have been kinder. The coroner assured me that John never felt anything, that whatever it was had been instantaneous. When Jennifer found him, he was lying on his sofa, Pippen quietly beside him. She thought he was asleep. There was nothing disturbed and no sign of a struggle. He still had on his hospital identification bracelet from the previous day's procedure.

I asked about an autopsy and the coroner said she would let me know if it would be necessary. I told them which mortuary and gave all my contact information. I let my ex and Megan know that I was going to my condo and that they could come there. I dropped off my friend at our downtown office, forgetting that her car was at the main hospital, and drove home.

Soon one of my friends was at the door with coffee, paper products, and enough cake and cookies to last a year.

"I just had to come," she said. "I went through the store just grabbing things!"

She had been with me through it all and I was grateful to see her. Then the doorbell rang with a floral delivery, my work colleagues sent over a catered meal for supper, and the phone calls began.

One call was from the coroner. She said that they would not do an autopsy because of John's extensive, well documented health history.

"What if we want an autopsy?" I asked.

She explained that insurance would not cover it, that it would have to be done by a private company, and it would require $5,000 cash up front.

"I can't do that," I said.

Again she showed her kindness when she commented, "He's been through so much, I'd hate to do that to his body."

All we could think was that it had to do with the heart procedure done less than 24 hours previously. John had had blood clots before, even a pulmonary embolism, which could cause death instantly.

The mortuary called next and scheduled a meeting for us the next day at 10 a.m. John's father and his wife arrived and soon after, my daughter and her husband.

Earlier, while sitting on the curb of the driveway, I'd said to Emily, "Well, you're up."

She looked at me, and I continued, "John and I both told you that you were to do his eulogy." She nodded.

My minister friend, who had supported me through the years and had tried to help John, was next. He would do the "message" part of the service. He also helped me think through how we might possibly have a service in the midst of COVID-19. My parents had a family plot at a lovely cemetery outside of town that could accommodate an outside service.

I don't remember anything more about that evening. Megan and her husband stayed with me and I slept. I never cried.

Pippen

I O

After July 23

A FEW OF US participated in the "family viewing" on Saturday morning. John would be cremated and his ashes scattered in the creeks at Litchfield at a later time. Jennifer, Megan, and John's father had picked his clothes—a favorite shirt, jeans, and his worn garnet Carolina cap. I only took a quick look, knowing he would have hated this. All I could think about was him waking up in a sunny field somewhere and saying, *Why is my shirt tucked in? Where are my shades? And where the hell is my phone?!*

"I struggle and arise" was the tattoo John had on his forearm and the message we placed on his marker. More than 200 people stood in the noon sun on a July Sunday to honor him. A bagpiper led in the small family procession. I followed the minister, holding my older granddaughter's hand. We wanted to have Pippen with us but decided she'd be happier at "Auntie Em's Camp for Wild Girls," which John called it when she stayed with Emily during his hospitalizations. My minister friend concluded the thirty-minute service by singing "The Lord's Prayer" a capella.

The following days we cleared out John's apartment. We did the majority of it on Monday while people were still in town to help. I don't remember much of anything but focusing on getting it done. Pippen went home with Megan. Jennifer and I finished it up the rest of the week as a few close guy friends came to get his watches, pocketknives, and shoes—he had quite a collection of each. His dialysis nurse came to get all the equipment and supplies. I picked cucumbers, peppers, an eggplant, and a watermelon from his garden.

Then I took a month's leave of absence from work.

A lot of the time I felt gratitude, and even some relief, that John wasn't suffering anymore and struggling to live. So many times the past year I had come to his apartment, almost daily, with a sense of dread and even guilt.

I felt so inadequate to address all his needs. I lived so frugally. I worried about money all the time. I didn't have a real "home" he could come to when he might need more care in the future. I didn't cook and bring him homemade meals. Mostly, I couldn't fix a healthcare system to make things better for him. All I could do was walk Pippen, run errands for him, and keep trying. It was a dark tunnel to which I saw no end.

I wished only that I could know his last thoughts. Jennifer had stayed with him until 9:30. She had left because she wasn't feeling well. She said they'd driven out to pick up supper and laughed a lot. His friends had told me that he was group-texting and joking with them that night until around 10:30. I couldn't understand. I prayed for a sign, for him to let me know he was OK.

It wasn't until the next week that I contacted the Charleston transplant center. Surprise, surprise, his coordinator had left days before John's final procedure and no one was actively following his case. I asked for the transplant nephrologist, who had given us so much hope and whom we'd never met in person. He called me quickly and was again most helpful—sad and sorry and shocked. He would have the cardiologist who did the last procedure contact me. When I said that we'd never heard the report from Behavioral Health and didn't know if John would have been approved, he was again surprised and said, "She was good with proceeding. He was approved."

It took a second for that to sink in, and then I was crying. So much, that we had all pushed so hard for. . .and yet it was not to be.

The cardiologist called next, and he was equally surprised. He had not even known that we had wanted the last procedure done in Greenville and said he would have been happy for John's cardiologist, whom he knew well, to have done it here. He could think of no reason for John's sudden death. Everything had gone well and all John's heart functions were within normal ranges. No one had answers.

I had so much anger at the Charleston pulmonologist, which I'd held from the beginning. I emailed a letter to Patient Relations, asking that it be sent to the director of the transplant program. By the next day, the director called me. He had no answers either, but he listened. He asked if he could have the pulmonologist call me and I said, "I never want to speak to him again."

The pulmonologist called me anyway—twice—leaving messages, which I heard as defensive condescension. I'm sure my anger was unmerited, that this doctor was trying to give John the best medical chance possible, but that last trip was just one more thing that made it all harder for him. Except for the perfect time with his sister at the beach and the selfie that became her permanent Facebook profile picture.

Megan's coordinator had called her, too. Her committee had met and approved her to be John's living donor–on the day he was found dead.

Jennifer and I went to Megan's the following Saturday. At the neighborhood pool watching the girls swim, I saw a huge yellow butterfly dancing near the pool. There were no trees or vegetation near, just concrete. I noted that as odd. Then I realized I had my sign.

"Thank you," I whispered to John.

Yet my mind was always questioning. *What was he thinking?* He was always thinking, non-stop. His sharp, active mind could never pause.

He was spent. He didn't know how he could keep going another day. Maybe he couldn't face another transplant. I knew he didn't want to take his sister's kidney. Maybe his spirit finally sought a way out. I searched his cell phone for clues. Maybe he'd just wanted a break from his reality, for even a few hours. *Which disease had killed him?*

I thought about how he'd gotten to be with all his friends recently at the lake. About the Charleston/beach time with his sister. About telling me he loved me. Did he know, too, that the end was near? Was he saying his goodbyes to us?

During that time, Megan called to tell me that John had come to her as a storm. She was out walking, talking with her father on the phone. It was a late August afternoon and a storm was brewing. Suddenly John the Storm was upon her in all his fury with pounding rain and darkness, breaking the connection and hanging up on their father. He was angry that we were all talking about him, analyzing him, going through his phone—and he didn't have a chance to tell his side. Then he calmed and was remorseful.

It was all I needed to hear.

It was later that night as I sat on my bed pondering, that I heard John say, *I'm sorry, Mama.* He had tried his best to stay alive for me, too.

John's first babysitter always said, "John's all boy." Never far from a ball, he was strong and quiet with a brilliant smile and a love for risks. Later, I thought of John as "all man," in the sense that he was fully human, in all the good and bad of that. John lived out his God-given free will, his freedom to be himself, fiercely. Never owning to something he could not believe, never giving in to less than his conviction of who he thought he was supposed to be, never giving up his own internal code. Some might call it pride. His spirit could not be broken—even in death itself.

I held onto a thought from Trappist monk Thomas Merton that the innermost center of ourselves belongs entirely to God and remains invincibly whole and undiminished. I believe that. I had no doubt but that God looked down and said, "It's time to come home, son." Knowing John's fear of death, God took him in unknowing sleep and welcomed him straight into his strong arms.

My older, godly friend always said that John was special. I asked her after his death exactly what she meant by that. She said, "Sometimes I get distinct messages. The first time I saw him at USC, I knew. I have a clear picture in my mind of his handsome face and lovely smile. Whatever the required accomplishment, it *was* and *will have* lasting action."

No matter how much I loved him, he was not mine, he was not ours.

John's girls

I I

The Following Year

I OBSERVED A YEAR of mourning. I was glad that COVID-19 kept things shut down for a good part of that time. I rested and read, did therapy, exercised, prayed and meditated, and finally started writing even though I didn't want to. Trying to make some sense of it all.

In October, around John's birthday which would have been his thirty-seventh, eight of us traveled to Litchfield to scatter John's ashes in the creeks he loved. The boat was similar to the one in which he and the others almost drowned many years ago. (We, however, had four persons in it at a time, rather than eight.) We told many stories. I had my list of trivia questions: How many cars/jeeps did he have? How many did he wreck? How many times was he arrested? How many times was he hospitalized? No one could answer that one, not even me.

As part of our little "scattering" service, I read some of John's words (written in 2017):

> To say I'm lucky wouldn't really describe my life. I am lucky to have the family, friends, and community that I do. But to say I am alive because of luck would not be fair to my family, friends, doctors, nurses, or myself. At no point did we give up. My mom, especially, refused to accept the situation in which I found myself, to the point of facing fear, uncertainty, and pain to help me. Although I don't remember some of what happened when I was hospitalized, I will never forget the difference of being in the hospital with and without my family. It was absolute night and day, and I don't doubt I would have died without them. I'll never forget the friends who showed up while times were tough. When there was no music playing and no beer being served, they walked in with tears in their eyes to see me again, not knowing if it would be the last time.
>
> It didn't kill me, and it sure as hell didn't make me physically stronger, but I am a better person for it. If for no other reason than

having a better understanding of pain and fear and hope and family and love. I am thankful for my life and everyone in it.

Sometimes, though, the progress almost seems like part of the problem. I feel so much better, and things still won't fall into place. I can't seem to get the job, money, relationships, to catch up—the depression stops me. It still feels like every time I make some progress, there's something there to slap me back down.

Going forward nonetheless, I hope to make people aware of the often unseen and misunderstood conditions involving autoimmune diseases, and I intend to do everything I can to be an advocate for organ and tissue donation. If one person is able to donate an organ because of me, then I may have figured out why I was given a second chance. (Since John Got Sick, page 127)

I remembered things that the extended time of active mothering had given me: teaching him how to iron a dress shirt for his bank job; Sunday rides across Paris Mountain or "down to the country" when he had no energy to do anything else; buying weekly deli turkey, sliced Provolone, "good" bread, Cocoa Puffs, and Cheese-Itz—none of which I ate—plus snack packs of peanut butter crackers and granola bars for him to take to dialysis. I think of these things that I don't put in my cart now every time I go to the grocery store.

I miss my son. I miss him for all he was and for all he could have been. I miss his smile and his love for me. I hurt for the pain he suffered.

I do not miss going to Walgreen's to pick up prescriptions because John was not able, wondering how many, if there would be a screw up this time, or if insurance would not pay . . . John's prescriptions were not of the $10 variety. I have not been able to go into that Walgreen's since.

Neither do I miss agonizing over every cent I spent.

John's grief at his inability to live the life he wanted was huge. No matter how hard he fought, how hard he tried, he could not change it. Coupled with the fact that he'd beat death so many times and that he'd always been a rebel and a thrill seeker, it made for a sense of invincibility. I had prayed for years for him to come to some acceptance of his situation and I had begun to see it happening. I was privileged to see major changes occur, from his countless hours of having to rest and be still. He grew in wisdom and compassion, and he found himself being not only a great storyteller but also a published author.

For all the times John could have died—and near-miraculously didn't—people said, "God saved him for a reason." John wished many times to be clued in to what that reason was.

One friend gave me a valuable gift in writing,

> "I have thought many times, 'He must be here for a reason.' And in a death as mysterious and beautiful as his life, the reason is revealed— it is us. As I look around, I see people gathered in the shade of trees, some in dappled sunlight and some in the blinding light of noonday, and family seated under a tent. I see very young and very old and every age in between. I see all the many friends he made in life and all the family he loved so much and so loved him. His amazing life touched all of ours in some way and made us better and stronger for it. The reason is us."

In the days since his death, countless people told me how John had helped them. By providing a listening ear, understanding with compassion, or just by never giving up, amidst great pain and a decade of difficulty.

He irrevocably changed my life. I don't think I'm the only one.

John didn't get to finish his life here. He most definitely didn't get to live the life he wanted. So I must choose to live my life fully, to share all the gifts he afforded me, to tell his story. I hope his legacy, like a classic movie, will live on.

Ashes at Litchfield

12

Tributes

JOHN GREENE DIED ON July 23, 2020, in his apartment with his dog beside him. After ten-plus years of struggle, he is no longer sick.

For all the times John could have died—and near-miraculously didn't—people said, "God saved him for a reason." John wished many times to be clued in to what that reason was.

In the days since his death, countless people have told us how John had helped them. By providing a listening ear, understanding with compassion, or just by never giving up, amidst great pain and a decade of difficulty.

Outside at noon on a July Sunday, a couple of hundred friends and family gathered to remember John's life.

Eulogy

Emily Price, *friend*

It was philosopher Immanuel Kant who said, "You can judge the heart of a man by his treatment of animals." I believe that all of us here would agree that to be true; and I believe it was this statement that became a now familiar proverb, "You can tell a lot about a man by his dog."

John's dog, Pippen, is a prime example of his goodness. I've gotten to know her very well during John's monumental struggles with his illness and its many complications, especially over the last couple of years; there was a spell this past year when he was in and out of the hospital on a monthly basis, and Pip would come to what John branded, "Auntie Em's Camp for Wild Girls."

Pippen is *the* most loving dog I've ever met. She's so much like John. She's well adjusted; unassuming; constantly doting; the most wonderful companion. She plays remarkably well with others. She loved him fiercely, as he loved her; he could do no wrong, nor did he to her. and no matter what he was dealing with—including chronic and debilitating physical pain and exhaustion that kept him from doing much of anything at all—he made sure she was always well taken care of. He would still manage to get up and walk her when he could barely move; when money was basically nonexistent, he still fed her well, and supplied her with peanut butter bones. Her coat always shiny and supple; her face full of sweetness, love and innocence, no matter if she had just seen him taken out of their home they shared by medics for a hospital stay.

She loved him so much that when Wilson and John lived together, and they had their own couches they'd lie on with their dogs and talk for hours and hours, that Pippen the puppy would only chew up the cushions on Wilson's couch.

Wilson's favorite memories of John—of which there were many—were watching John raise her as a puppy. He valued that time he got to see the nurturer in John at work.

And when John passed away in his sleep on Thursday morning, he was found with Pippen lovingly by his side; with him until the very end, as he was also with her. He leaned on her for emotional support and she gave him so much joy. And when John and Pippen were found that fateful morning lying next to each other—she was calm, because she knew his ultimately insurmountable physical, mental and emotional struggles stemming from his disease were over.

I have no doubt his spirit stayed with her, scratching her ears, and assuring her that all was well; that all was better than it had been in a long, long, long time—since he'd known her—because John was finally free (which John was determined to be, no matter what).

Free of physical pain; free of the many ultimately immovable roadblocks life presented to him, that inhibited him from living up to his wildly uncategorical potential.

John's extraordinarily large spirit will stay with all of us. We must remember to channel it. He will be here with us, now and always. It's through our memories of John, and the lessons that his life—including the premature end of it—that will ensure that he did, indeed, live up to his potential here on this earth. He taught all of us a great deal about life, struggle and he especially taught us all about strength.

John was a fighter in every sense of the word. He was strong as hell. He stared death in the face over and over and over again, and he never gave up.

He never even thought about giving up, even when those of us surrounding him didn't see how there was anything else to do but submit to the circumstances of his physical health.

They say a cat has nine lives, but John has approximately 732—that's an estimation— because I lost count. And now, he is experiencing his BEST life. He made it, y'all. He made it to eternal greatness, for which his most notably spirited of spirits was surely destined. He was, indeed, a local legend.

John was not necessarily the most reasonable person; he was stubborn as they come. And those tendencies are exactly why he survived as long as he did, and we need to remember to channel those things into our own lives when we're presented with difficulties—especially the biggest one's life can challenge us with. Even when things seem unreasonable, sometimes we have to say, "No. Not today. I'm not done here yet"—because life is far, far bigger than reason.

About six months ago, I asked John why he had always embraced risk. Why at times, from my perspective, he chose "living on the edge" instead of living safely. He was not too keen on taking advice from others. He told me that he had thought about that a lot (because he thought about EVERYTHING a lot, even his seemingly unwise choices). He said it was because he just had to figure everything out for himself. I asked him if he had heard the quote, also from Immanuel Kant, that "Happiness is not an ideal of reason, but of imagination," because it reminded me of John's approach to life. He hadn't, but he said, "That makes a lot of sense. I think I'll go read some Kant."

By the way, if you did not know this side of John, he was a brilliant intellectual, and very easily bored. One way he passed the time while disabled was to read (he was always a voracious reader), but he would read philosophy and politics, even when in a brain fog on a plethora of prescription drugs and battling exhaustion from sleepless nights, struggling to get through an almost unbearable routine of dialysis.

He had a huge imagination—one that was well matched with the enormity of his spirit. We talked a lot about philosophy, spirituality, psychology, poetry . . . he loved all of it. He was an extraordinarily deep thinker, and you could see that in any given moment in his giant, deep eyes.

But back to my prior point about John's pursuit of happiness not being through reason, but through imagination: that leads me to a story one of his best friends, Taylor, told me.

The summer after their junior year in high school, they were at Litchefield with their crew. John and Taylor had fake IDs, and they got the idea to go get some tattoos together (which were not even legal in South Carolina at the time). Nobody else wanted to do it, but the two of them drove to the North Carolina border and got these tattoos (John's was on his back). They thought they were the coolest dudes on the planet for about six months . . . but six months in, they were hanging out again, and looked at each other and were like, "What the hell did we do? Why did we do this?!" They hated their tattoos pretty early on, but had a good laugh about it, of course.

But it was just the other day that Taylor was with his wife as he glimpsed his tattoo in the mirror and said, "Hey, babe. This is actually the first time that this tattoo has actually made me smile." Because it finally means something to him. He finally found the reason behind that tattoo from their youthful adventure.

Perhaps John's penchant for acting out of imagination (because the reason will come later) has some weight to it. Perhaps we should all remember that approach to life more often, so we can live BIG lives; BIG lives like John's are destined to have meaning.

So many things came easily to John—a lot of times, it seemed like he didn't have to try to excel. So many exceptional abilities just came to him naturally—and I think that this fostered some boredom in John most of us don't have to combat on a daily basis, and which likely confused a lot of people.

This natural ability included athletics, as he was an exceptional natural athlete. Another one of John's best friends, Kirkley, told me one of his favorite memories of John: their freshman year of high school, they both made Greenville High's wrestling team. John pinned a two times state champion from Liberty the first time he ever got on the mat, in the first period. In response, the guy John pinned (again, without much wrestling experience to speak of), stormed into Greenville High's gym, busted out a window, and was suspended for the rest of the season.

John was effortlessly COOL. "Greene was just so cool. He was always cool to me, early in life. He was *That* guy. He had that thing—stuff that stood out to me. We were peers, but I always thought he was so much cooler than me," Kirkley also told me.

I agree wholeheartedly. He was a bit of a legend. He was almost untouchable. He always had the nice cologne; the cool, fresh threads; the magnetic, giant smile. The dimples that broke 2,000 hearts (again, that's an approximation, as I lost count on that, too). I remember in college when one girl told me "Oh, John Greene?! He walked around the halls of high school like he was a *god*. Everyone adored him." I never told John that that was said to me. . .but I guess I will give you that one today, buddy.

John was wickedly funny—and he enjoyed a good prank. As I struggled to live up to the task of eulogizing an actual "legend," as it was John's request that I do so—I think this was his way of getting in the last word and laugh after the many years of our friendship I spent lecturing him. I was writing this over the weekend and I could hear him whispering through the trees, "Well, you always liked to lecture and tell me what's what, so take your best shot, girl!"

Point taken, John. Point taken.

John touched many lives, as is evidenced here today by this attendance of you all. He was deeply good, not just evidenced in the nature of his dog, Pip and their companionship—but John kept his best friends for life. He changed our lives, and those of the kids he coached soccer to; the patients he met while driving them to dialysis; the homeless people he helped by sourcing tents, food, and supplies. John wanted to get well to go to graduate school for psychology and become a therapist; he had been researching programs over the past year. He is loved by so many people, because he loved all of us with his full self. He gave us all he had. He fought to live for a decade so that he could continue to be here and love us HARD.

Lastly, the thing John would want us to remember going forward is that we can all be organ donors. You can join your state's registry online at organdonor.gov or at your local DMV. It's easy, and I would like you all to consider leaving the gift of life in John's memory. I urge you to commit to living a life SO big, it cannot be contained by one livelihood, one body, like John.

The Reverend Dr. Stephen C. Clyborne

"Constant Companions"—Isaiah 43:1–3a; Jeremiah 31:3b; Romans 8:31–39

It was Robert Browning who wrote,

> *I walked a mile with Pleasure. She chatted all the way,*
> *But left me none the wiser for all she had to say.*
> *I walked a mile with Sorrow, and ne'er a word said she.*

But, oh, the things I learned from her when Sorrow walked with me.

John Greene walked more than just a mile with sorrow. Sorrow was his companion for the last ten years of his life. At the age of twenty-six, this rare autoimmune disease struck out of nowhere and threatened to end his journey of life many times. I cannot count the number of times I heard Allison say during John's arduous struggles, "I just don't know how he is still alive." Through all his extended hospital stays, his surgeries, the transplant, and all the complications that resulted, sorrow was his constant companion - sorrow that he could not thrive the way he wanted to; sorrow that he was not able to work and play, relax and plan the way other people in his stage of life could; sorrow that lingers after physical and emotional trauma; sorrow that feels like a dull ache even when it does not feel like a sharp pain. For the past ten years, sorrow was his companion.

Even when he felt relatively good, even when he was able to work and play and enjoy his life - even then, especially then, in the back of his mind was this underlying sorrow. "It's always there," he told me one day when we were having lunch together. "It's always in the back of my mind no matter where I go or what I do, no matter how good I feel or how bad I feel. It's always there." And it was. He walked more than a mile with sorrow.

But sorrow was not his only companion. Love was another companion that was always there - the love of a devoted mother who would have given her life for him, and almost did; the love of a father and sister and other family members who hurt when he hurt and shared this journey with him; the love of a girlfriend who took such good care of him until the very end; the love of special friends like Emily, the guys standing here with the family, and countless others who believed in him and supported him; the love of his dog, Pippen, who gave John joy in his darkest moments; the love of a whole community of people who prayed him through so many of his heartaches and setbacks; all of whom were expressions of a love so deep and so wide that it could only be explained by the greatest love of all—the love of God.

In writing to the Romans, Paul assured us that nothing can ever separate us from the great love of God, expressed supremely in Jesus Christ our Lord—not hardship, or distress . . . death, life, angels, rulers, things present, things to come, powers, height, depth, nor anything else in all creation, will be able to separate us from the love of God in Christ Jesus our Lord.

In my lunch conversation with John at Panera Bread almost three years ago now, when John told me that "it's always there," he said something else that stuck with me. He said, "I hope one day I'll get through this and won't have to carry this around with me anymore." And Thursday morning when John closed his eyes in death, that day finally came.

John certainly walked more than a mile with sorrow. But sorrow was not his only companion. Love walked with him, too. That explains why sorrow did not stop him in his tracks. That is why John kept fighting and kept going because, as the prophets said, when he passed through the waters, Love was with him; and when he passed through the rivers, they did not sweep over him. When he walked through the fire, he was not consumed. When sorrow threatened to pull him down along the way, love kept him going—your love for him and God's love for him. In the last ten years of his life, sorrow was his constant companion. But not anymore. Sorrow finally left him, but love did not. And the same love that was John's constant companion in his life is our constant companion in his death. God's love for us is everlasting. It has no end, which is why Paul said that not even death can separate us from the great love of God in Christ Jesus our Lord.

John traveled more than a mile with at least two companions—sorrow and love. There came a time when sorrow gave out of strength and dropped out of John's life for good, but love never did, and love never will. Thanks be to God. Amen.

Megan Greene Roberts, *sister*

John Garrison Greene defied simple descriptions or explanations.

From the time he could walk, maybe even before, my little brother was cool. He wore a three-piece suit with a bowtie and matching sunglasses to Easter church when he was four. He was a natural athlete with a ready half-smile and a twinkle in his eye. He was the guy you want to sit next to at a party—or a funeral—because he was the king of the witty aside. He had an opinion about everything and a sharp way to share it.

He was a natural storyteller. (If you haven't read his writing, you should, you'll love it.) I can't tell you how many times I asked him to recount the stories of the summer he spent replacing sewer pipes with Ryan. He knows things about roaches no one should. Just this past Wednesday morning, we were walking to the hospital in downtown Charleston together and saw a worker opening a manhole. John said, "That's when you want to go ahead and tuck your pants into your boots. Those suckers are everywhere." He was going in for a heart procedure, he was nervous, and as usual, the patient was the one cracking me up.

He was a paradox. As lacking in self-assurance as he was confident, thoughtful and judgmental, boisterous, and shy. He never met a superstition he didn't follow. He was smart, creative, kind, brave, sensitive, and stubborn. That word keeps coming up, and we laugh because it's true, and because when we say it, we're talking about everything from his personal sense of integrity to his obstinance. If John set his mind to something, that's the way it was. And thank God for that. John flat out did not want to be sick, (on my thirtieth birthday I had to catch him and drag him back when he tried to escape his Duke hospital room by Greyhound bus) and his stubbornness gave us ten extra years with him.

Early in his illness he had the words "I struggle and arise" tattooed on his arm. That's what it's been ever since. He demonstrated almost impossible strength for us all. He fought so hard, and he fought hard to hide his pain for all of us.

He was so grateful for his friends, many of whom have been by his side since preschool. You were his brothers, and sisters. You were his world.

He loved his dog. He loved his family. Especially the members we've lost, especially his nieces—you were his joy; especially his parents—you gave him everything—your time, your patience, your hope, your figurative hearts and literal kidney; especially me.

He is finally finished with the pain. Because of the way he protected us, I'm so thankful that the pain isn't what I'll remember. I'll hear his raspy voice, sure, but I'll hear it laughing. It's been ringing in my head for days. The different laughs he makes when I say something stupid, or when a friend texts a crazy picture, or when he lets his nieces paint his toenails, or when he's telling a great story from better times, even the summer of the roaches.

Call me stubborn, but I'll remember my brother laughing.

He loved us well.

He struggled and arose.

May he rest in peace and rise in glory. Amen.

Smith Brownell, *friend*

John Garrison Greene was many things; a son, a brother, a lady's man, a best friend, an athlete, a teammate, a friend to many, a brother from another mother (thank you, Alison and Vic), unfortunately a patient (although not patient at times himself, lol), a fast driver, a trash talker and instigator, a hat man, a fisherman, a Carolina football lover (again, unfortunately, lol), a guy with many hairdos. People loved John and wanted to be around him. His presence was always welcome! Wherever I went; "Oh yeah, your boy John Greene, he's cool as s**t, bring him along." He was a crowd pleaser and easy on the eyes, to the ladies.

There are too many things that come to mind when I think of the name, John Greene. I think of his smile and now raspy voice and laugh. I think of an old friend and younger times at Litchfield Beach more than recent years because that was when he was happy living life—chasing girls, playing soccer, fishing and clamming in the Yuk Yacht, kicking the football, and getting in good trouble. Yes, John and I got in a fair share of situations, but we always had fun doing it and we always had each other's backs. Not to say without some regret here and there along the way, but John was there for me and I like to think I was there for him, especially in times of hardships and struggles.

In fact, the last time I saw John we argued with each other over the fireworks show on the Fourth of July at Lake Hartwell, to the point that it almost got physical, and only to wake up the next morning and laugh about it and brush it off with no hard feelings. We didn't hold grudges on one another, not like it would do either of our stubborn heads any good.

I know John felt low and unmotivated a lot once he got sick. I tried to keep pushing him because I knew he could push through with his stubbornness and tough mentality. John was strong willed, and I always looked up to him for that. I know he wanted to study more, to be strong again, to travel, to just be happy and in zero pain, and in love. We all wanted that for him, too. At times I honestly did not know what was going through his head. I'd push him via conversation, usually over the phone and as much as I could in person in the later years of his life. We would argue here and there but both knew the initial conversation was coming from love of a friend and brother. I remember telling him one day when he was down to "take the word 'can't' out of your brain, Greene," and to get the hell up and go do it, John! That was usually the kind of guy he was, but I didn't realize how down he'd get at times, nor did I understand it.

We all miss John but are happy is no longer struggling with his disease or his demons. We all face tough times, but I can say John was honestly the strongest person I know and fought like hell for years to get better. He wanted to get healthy and be "normal," but always got held back it seemed. We all slip and fall and try to get up again and again throughout life, only to sometimes fall even further. For the fight that John Garrison Greene put up, I will gladly assign an A+ to a friend and brother. He will remain that, in his memory and his soul that lives on through us when we search for truth and answers.

Sean Smith, *friend*
(received more than a year after John's death)

I just had a little surgery and had to spend a few hours in a recovery room. It was not fun and all I could think about was how many hours, months, and years John had to spend in *such* worse pain, boredom, and stress. He was an absolute warrior. He is no longer suffering and that brings me comfort. He's always on my mind.

Jennifer Childs, *girlfriend*

How do you eulogize someone who meant everything to you? Someone who impacted your life in the deepest way imaginable? How do I put into words what John, the only man I've ever been in love with, meant to me or how he inspired all of us time and time again? Well, the answer is I can't, but I will do my best to honor him by sharing some of my favorite memories.

I think my heart loved him long before the rest of me knew it. I honestly didn't even realize that I was completely in love with John until someone else pointed it out to me. I had never loved anyone like that before. He was my first love. Not that my life was meaningless before him, but it wasn't as vibrant before he became a part of it. We spent thousands of hours together over the years but unfortunately, some of the closest people to us had no idea—a regrettable decision now. In the days that followed that wretched, life-altering moment when I discovered his lifeless body in his apartment, many memories were shared among family members. I remember I was huddled with Megan, whom I had met face-to-face exactly once before John died, trading stories. I had provided an alternate version of just about every anecdote we exchanged throughout the better part of a decade when she paused, a thoughtful look on her face, and proclaimed, "You were a ghost! You were there all along and we had no idea." I nodded in silence as

I watched her let it sink in that I had been in the shadows all that time and often a source of his happiness.

This was not the first time I had heard this. I'd heard versions of this sentiment from Allison, other family members, and some of John's closest friends. It was one of my biggest arguments with John over the years; why was he so private about our relationship when I had consistently been a part of his life, and arguably one of the most important people he had by his side the last fourteen months of it? Once we found out his kidney was failing, I stopped pressing on this issue. After all, he had much bigger challenges ahead of him, and posting pictures about the status of our relationship was trivial. My broken heart lifts a tiny bit more each time one of his family members or friends tells me how comforted they are to know that he wasn't always alone all those times during all those years.

When Allison asked me to write about my favorite memory of John, I had a breakdown. How could I possibly choose from the myriad of memories that stretched back a decade? I could talk about our first date when he proudly showed me pictures of his nieces, one of whom was just born. I could tell the story of how he first told me he loved me right before my birthday one year. I could talk about how wonderful he was to me when I got laid off from a job I hated in 2017, and how he encouraged and helped me that entire year. I could talk about how excited he was to show me everything he learned in his home dialysis training and how proud and hopeful I felt watching him expertly stick very large needles in his arm by himself. This led to me sitting with him almost every single day during home dialysis, and it's time I'm incredibly grateful we had together. I could talk about how I begged him not to give up during the March of 2020 hospitalization, telling him I'd be right by his side to help, but I needed him to fight. He promised me he would fight and confessed he wasn't ready to die. I could mention the days and nights I spent with him in the hospital—the time where we acted silly in the cafeteria as I pushed him around in a wheelchair, or the night I slept at the hospital with him when we watched Clemson almost lose to Ohio State during the Fiesta Bowl, or that evening spent half-watching "The Sandlot" while clutching his hand in the ICU when I witnessed him have a PTSD episode— all of these moments deeply bonded us. I could write about the neighborhood walks I encouraged him to go on with Pip and myself, many of which ended with us getting ice cream. Or there are many date nights filled with sushi dinners, movies, and cooking together side-by-side. The car rides that were filled with music of artists we taught each other about. The holidays we spent together—Thanksgiving night eating take out, Christmas afternoon when we shopped for gifts for his family and ran into a mini horse on Main Street, and New Year's Day when we hooked up speakers a friend gave him and listened to Bob Marley while he cooked us a late brunch. I could mention the garden we started together or the time we assembled furniture for his new dialysis room with ease and high-fived ourselves afterward, laughing in glee that we "didn't kill each other." Or how we always talked non-stop whenever I traveled out of town—it was sometimes during these conversations that he shared profoundly personal stories about himself. I could give countless examples of his quick wit, intelligence, and athleticism—like the time he got down on the sidewalk and showed one of my friends how to correctly do a push-up. I could tell you about the time he and the nurse broke into his iPhone when he woke up in the hospital in April of 2020 because he couldn't stand another second without talking to me. I remember I received his call when I was outside walking. I had to sit down on the curb in front of a stranger's yard because I was so relieved to hear his voice. He was a little loopy so the nurse got on the phone with me and explained that he woke up asking for me and would not stop until they figured out his passcode and found my name in his contacts to call. I remember she told me, "You must be pretty special because he's been asking about you since he woke up." I was so over-whelmed with love for him at that moment that I cried tears of joy on the side of the road. We FaceTimed several times the rest of the day when he was more coherent. He was weepy and emotional and kept making fun of himself saying, "I'm so emo," which made me laugh. Perhaps this is my second favorite story because he was much softer after that last hospitalization. I believed things really looked up for us at that time. We operated as a team from then on, falling into an easy, harmonious rhythm. We were even making tentative post-transplant plans.

There are hundreds more accounts I could lend about my favorite person, some of them so precious to me that only the two of us will ever know about them. If I forced myself to choose only one, it would probably be this next rollercoaster of a story. On May 2, 2019, we had a spectacular row. He was unrecognizable to me during an argument that escalated so quickly, it left me spinning and devastated by some of the things he said to me. The erratic behavior and hurtful words towards me were so unlike him. We hadn't spoken for two weeks when suddenly, I received a message from him in the

Duke hospital. He was basically telling me he was going to die. I was standing on a beach in Alabama surrounded by live music and happy festival-goers when I read his message. It was such a bizarre backdrop to receiving the news I never wanted to hear. I found myself unable to breathe even on the wide-open shore next to the Gulf Coast. Scared and confused, I pressed him for more details. Due to the one-hour time difference and the fact I didn't receive or respond to the message until nighttime, I didn't hear back from him until the next morning. I tossed and turned all night, my mind racing with thoughts of the worst possible outcomes. And then a lightbulb went off when I realized this must be related to that night two weeks prior when he acted so differently with me. I knew something couldn't have been right. I knew he'd never behave that way towards me unless something else was going on. I didn't realize it at the time, but it made sense now. I had to see him, but I was three states away and didn't have my car. Finally, he responded and elaborated on what he'd said to me the night before. I'll never forget the message I sent next. I told him, "I love you and I need you to be okay." We talked non-stop the next two days and nights about many things. The tone of his messages seemed to be a little lighter now that we were in sync and he had me back in his good graces—he was even flirting with me like normal, which made me smile. That he could be so himself, like nothing was wrong when in fact everything was wrong, was so John. The only thing greater than his determination was his need to be normal. We both left on Monday—me from Alabama, him from North Carolina—and I went straight to his apartment the minute I got back to my car. Though insanely terrifying and seeming like a bad dream from which we wanted to wake up, that night, one of many we spent together throughout the years, might be my most memorable and sacred. Things changed for us after that night. As we clung to one another for hours, apologies were made, tears were shed, fears and phobias were communicated, and patterns of behavior I'd observed for years finally made sense. His walls were finally down. I truly saw him and understood him that day. HE mattered to me and all I ever wanted for him was for him to be happy, even if it meant I wasn't a part of it. I am still so grateful that he deemed me worthy of being a part of it.

I know I have a long road ahead of putting back together the shattered pieces of my heart. When I think about living the rest of my life without him, I physically ache with sadness. As the absence of him grows familiar, I'm comforted by two things: John is happy and content now that his mind and body are free from anguish, and he will continue to matter to me and all of the other people whose lives he impacted.

John, your story is an important one and no one can deny the mental and physical strength you exhibited for a decade. You are fearless and we are in awe of you. Thank you for trusting me to be a part of your story. You are my favorite. I miss you and I love you.

Friends

Frequently Asked Questions for Donors

What does it mean to be a living kidney donor?

A living kidney donor is someone who volunteers to give one of his or her two kidneys to someone whose kidneys are poorly functioning and may be receiving or nearing the need to receive dialysis treatments.

Can a person live a normal life with only one kidney?

Yes. The remaining kidney of a healthy donor will grow stronger. After donation, most donors will have seven times as much kidney function as is necessary to avoid the need for dialysis.

Who can be a living kidney donor?

Anyone who has normal kidney function, no disease that could be transmitted through donation and no major health problems that could damage the remaining kidney can be considered as a potential donor.

Does a living donor need to be related to the recipient of the kidney?

Although a kidney from a relative may be a better match and last longer in the body of a kidney transplant recipient, anyone who is interested in donation and meets the above criteria can undergo evaluation. Often a living donor is a spouse, step-relation, workmate, classmate, someone with whom they worship, or even a stranger.

What if I am not a match with the recipient of my kidney?

You are still able to donate anonymously to a stranger on behalf of your recipient. Your recipient would then get a kidney from a stranger as part of a donor "swap" or "exchange" process.

Can I donate a kidney to a stranger in need?

Absolutely! Altruistic individuals are welcome to be considered as kidney donors and are regarded as heroes by our team.

What can I expect during my evaluation as a donor?

Once you have been screened by a living donor coordinator by telephone, you will be asked to have blood and urine studies. If they are acceptable, you will be scheduled for a full-day appointment. During your evaluation day appointment, you will receive extensive education and meet with a team of transplant professionals.

Will the potential recipient of my kidney know if I call to consider donating my kidney?

No. Your health information will be kept confidential. Only if you desire that we share your information with your recipient will we do so.

What if I change my mind?

At any point during the evaluation process, you are permitted to change your mind and not move forward with the donation process. In addition, you will have the opportunity to meet with an independent living donor advocate who will make sure that you feel properly educated and not under any pressure to donate.

What other options does my loved one have if I choose not to donate them a kidney?

Your loved one could opt to receive dialysis therapy for his or her kidney disease, receive a kidney from a different living donor or wait for a deceased donor kidney.

What are the benefits for my loved one to receive a living donor kidney rather than a kidney from a deceased donor?

The waiting time to receive a kidney from a deceased donor can take as long as eight years. In comparison, a transplant from a live donor can be obtained sooner and limit the amount of time that your loved one may need dialysis treatments. Living donor transplant surgery can be scheduled when the recipient is in the peak of his or her health. Also, living donor kidneys tend to last longer than deceased donor kidneys.

What are the risks of kidney donation?

Kidney donation is major surgery and thus possible complications such as bleeding, infection, and blood clots, and complications from anesthesia could occur. Even though your remaining kidney will grow stronger after donation, you will have a slight reduction in your overall level of kidney function after donating one of your kidneys. Your blood pressure might increase slightly years after donation. Women who become pregnant after donation have a slightly increased risk of preeclampsia compared to women who have not donated kidneys. During your evaluation for donation, new health issues may be identified that may require further treatment.

What expenses are involved with kidney donation?

In most cases, your kidney recipient's insurance should cover all medical expenses associated with your evaluation and surgery. You will be seen and evaluated by a transplant social worker and financial counselor before donation who will provide more information for your specific circumstances.

How long does kidney donation surgery take?

On average, kidney donation surgery takes around two hours.

How long will I remain in the hospital after donating a kidney?

Typically, a kidney donor will go home from one to two days after surgery.

How long does it take to fully recover from kidney donation surgery?

Most patients will fully recover from kidney donation surgery in four to six weeks.

Frequently Asked Questions for Recipients

How do I get on the waiting list to receive a kidney transplant?

The kidney transplant process starts with making an appointment at a transplant center. This appointment can be made by you, your dialysis facility, your kidney specialist or another physician. During your visit, you will receive extensive education and be fully evaluated to ensure that a kidney transplant is a good option for you. Once you have successfully completed your evaluation, you will be placed on the waiting list.

How long will my initial appointment take?

When you are seen for evaluation for a kidney transplant, you will receive education, have X-rays and blood tests, and be seen by multiple members of the transplant team. Expect to be present for at least six hours.

What is a "deceased donor kidney"?

A deceased donor kidney is a kidney from someone who has previously expressed a desire to be an organ donor and has subsequently died. Most often, deceased donors are donors who have experienced "brain death" but still have a heartbeat and whose kidneys are working. Occasionally, deceased donor kidneys may be surgically recovered immediately after the donor's heart stops beating.

How long will I need to be on the waiting list before receiving a transplant?

The amount of time someone needs to wait for a kidney is quite variable, depending on your blood type, your immune system, the availability of a well-matched kidney and other factors. Most recipients will wait two to eight years for their kidney. If you are already receiving dialysis therapy, you will get credit for waiting for your transplant from the date you first started dialysis.

What is a "living donor kidney" transplant?

A living donor kidney transplant occurs when a healthy person chooses to give one of his or her two kidneys to you through surgical donation.

Who can be a living donor?

Anyone who has normal kidney function, no illnesses that can be transmitted to you and no illnesses that could destroy the remaining kidney can be considered as a donor.

Does a living donor need to be a relative?

Although a relative's kidney may be a better match and be expected to last longer in your body, a living donor kidney can come from a stranger or from anyone who loves you and is qualified to donate as above. This may, for example, include a spouse, step-relation, workmate, classmate or someone with whom you worship.

What if my donor is not a match?

Even if your donor does not match you because of your immune system or a difference in your blood types, your donor can still donate to a stranger anonymously on your behalf. You would then receive a stranger's kidney as part of a donor "swap" or "exchange" process.

What are the drawbacks to receiving a kidney transplant?

Kidney transplantation is a major surgery with potential complications. After a kidney transplant, you will be required to take medications that help to prevent rejection for the rest of your life. These medications can be expensive and cause side effects. You will also be required to have multiple follow-up visits and blood tests to monitor your kidney function after surgery. Over time, the frequency of these visits will decrease.

How long does a kidney transplant surgery take?

On average, a kidney transplant surgery takes around two hours.

How long will I remain in the hospital?

On average, the recipient of a kidney transplant will go home three to five days after surgery.

Will I be able to stop dialysis treatments after surgery?

Although dialysis is occasionally required after transplant surgery while awaiting your kidney to "wake up," most patients do not require any further dialysis after surgery.

How long does it take to recover from transplant surgery?

Most patients will fully recover from transplant surgery in four to six weeks.

How long does a typical kidney transplant function?

Typically, a kidney transplant will last five to fifteen years. Once your transplanted kidney fails, you would need to resume dialysis therapy. You may qualify for a second transplant if necessary.

Resources

National Kidney Foundation www.kidney.org

Donate Life America www.donatelife.net

FAVOR Greenville www.favorgreenville.org

CPSIA information can be obtained
at www.ICGtesting.com
Printed in the USA
LVHW081429190322
713746LV00005B/18